Hope
WHEN THE
RIVER RAGES

A Journey of Risk and Rescue,
Struggle and Strength, Fear and Faith

NANCY KALTENBERGER

LifeSong Publishers
P.O. Box 183
Somis, CA 93066
www.lifesongpublishers.com

Published by LifeSong Publishers
P.O. Box 183, Somis, CA 93066-0183
805-655-5644
www.lifesongpublishers.com

Unless otherwise noted, all Bible quotations used in this study are taken
from the New International Version Bible.

Scripture taken from the THE HOLY BIBLE, NEW INTERNATIONAL
VERSION. Copyright 1973, 1978, 1984 International Bible Society. Used
by permission of Zondervan Bible Publishers.

"Rejoice in the Lord" lyrics by Ron Hamilton. Copyright 1978 by Majesty
Music, P.O. Box 6524, Greenville, So. Carolina 29606.
info@majestymusic.com. Used by Permission.

Cover and chapter head design by Jon Walusiak at Design Point.

Library of Congress Cataloging-in-Publication Data

Kaltenberger, Nancy, 1948-
  Hope when the river rages / by Nancy Kaltenberger.— 1st ed.
     p. cm.
  ISBN-13: 978-0-9718306-7-7 (pbk.)
1. Hope—Religious aspects—Christianity. 2. Consolation. 3. Suffering—
Religious aspects—Christianity. 4. Kaltenberger, Nancy, 1948- 5. Near-
death experiences—Religious aspects—Christianity. I. Title.
BV4638.K35 2006
248.8'6—dc22
                          2006004393

Printed in the United States of America

To my children-
Thank you for believing in me.

"He reached down from on high
and took hold of me;
he drew me out of deep waters."
Psalm 18:16

Hope
When the River Rages

Acknowledgments..............

To Laurie Donahue. You have been so much more than an editor; you've been my friend. Your gentle shepherding of this entire project has been enlightening, encouraging, affirming, and inspirational. Thank you for partnering with me to bring this story full circle. I am honored to have served alongside you.

To the wonderful people of Grace Community Church who urged me, supported me, and prayed for me. You are a group of people who welcomed me, embraced me, and held me during my deepest valleys and I will be forever grateful.

To Michael. You brought me logic seasoned with love, advice sweetened with assurance, and help sprinkled with hope. Like Aaron and Hur who were ever attentive to the needs of Moses, you held my arms up when I had no strength of my own. Thank you for listening to me, believing in me, and helping me.

To Matt. Thank you for your inspiration. I am proud to call you Son. I am privileged to call you Pastor. Words cannot express what your ministry has meant to me, how I've grown under your teaching, and what an awesome blessing it has been to be able to watch God working in and through your life.

To Mandy. You are the daughter I thought I would never have. You are the best friend my soul longed for. You have been my champion, my defender, and my confidant. You taught me silliness, spontaneity, and laughter. You never once failed to show up on the sideline of my race track and cheer me on to victory. You are an amazing pot of gold and I am blessed to have been touched by your rainbow and light.

To my Dad. Thank you for the hope you instilled in me as a child. You truly made me believe I could go the distance. You are, and will always be, the best story-teller in the world!

To my Mom who taught me to always put my best foot forward. You have the gift of looking for the best in people. I thank you for seeing and encouraging the best in me.

To the many friends and loved ones who have touched my life, and been a part of my growing and learning journey. Thank you for coloring the pages of my storybook with your brilliant shades of love and laughter, influence and wisdom.

I am especially thankful to God Almighty who has seen fit to carry me through the storms of life. I am grateful for Your message of hope and humbled to be entrusted with sharing it with others.

PREFACE

HOPE is without a doubt, the most beautiful word in the English language. Our world is starving for just little doses of hope, little sprinkles of sunshine on otherwise dark and dreaded days. In a time when so many words are used like weapons that attack and destroy, this four letter word is truly one of the "good guys," one of the "best guys."

I've watched people throughout my life who didn't seem to know how to, or maybe were just afraid to, reach out and hope. Perhaps they came from a background where hope was never embraced. Maybe they were hurt; maybe at some point their dreams were shattered. Maybe disappointment, hardship or grief levied too great a toll. For whatever reason, they have lived their lives never daring to touch, grasp or stir hope on any level. The sadness, the emptiness and the void created by the absence of hope is not only destructive, it's debilitating.

Hoping and wishing, although very close to the same definitions in Webster's dictionary, are vastly different when they play out in our lives. We can buy a lottery ticket and put into motion the "wish'n, hope'n, and pray'n" philosophy captured in the lyrics of the old 50s song. We may even claim that we're believe'n we hold the winning ticket. There's certainly nothing wrong with positive thinking. Seeing the glass half full instead of half empty is the perception of a stable personality, not to mention a person who's easier to be around. But at the end of the day, that attitude, although admirable, is simply a "wishful thinking" state of mind. True HOPE takes on a much deeper definition. It becomes something alive in us, something that flows in and through us. It comforts us, holds us together, and gives us reason to go on. Hope in this life makes today bearable. Hope beyond this life carries us on wings as we face tomorrow.

I want to share hope with you. I know that as you read my story, there will be scores and scores of your own that will surface and beg to be told, to be shared. I know that my experiences will wane in light of the hopeful walk many of you have traveled in life. My heart's desire is not to one-up anyone, not to tell a story for shock value and most of all not to gain personal praise or admiration. My HOPE is that I will be able to ignite a fire, nudge, urge someone, somewhere to reach out and open the gifts that God has given them. My PURPOSE is to awaken dreams, visions, and missions long ago forsaken for lack of hope. My DESIRE is that you will see the Creator, the Savior who made the ultimate sacrifice for mankind in order for you to "live out" hope in your life. May God receive the glory, honor, and praise.

Nancy

ONE

WHITE WATER RAFTING

"I sought the Lord and He answered me;
He delivered me from all my fears." Psalm 34:4

*Cold...So Cold. Oh, dear Lord ...What happened?
...I'm in the water ...can't breathe! Help me! Can't see
...can't get my head up. What's on top of me ...I'm under
the raft ...Oh, dear God, help me ...I'm trapped ...Help me!
...Help me!*

Seemingly there was so much of life I hadn't lived, so
much I was pushing myself to experience. I had always
been sensible. I made sure to approach things in a logical,
safe and reasonable manner. I had been a mommy most of
my life. My children were my life. My thought processes,
my visions, my emotions, my priorities started and stopped
with what was best for my kids. Now, however, at the age
of 47, my body clock was striking every minute with a
painfully loud jolt. I was disillusioned by a recent divorce,
and the camera of my life was zooming in on 50, snapping
shot after shot so quickly I was beginning to loose myself
in the frame. I made resolutions to start taking risks, jump
into life, have fun, laugh more.

A dear friend suggested that my daughter, Mandy,

and I go on a white water rafting trip down the Poudre River in my home state of Colorado. Now, I'm not particularly strong or athletic. I'm not a great swimmer. Boats and rushing water are a little out of my comfort zone. But here, staring me in the face, was one of those "now or never" experiences that would pass me by if I sat down to weigh out all the reasons I should and should not go. I was determined to be spontaneous, daring and fun. I thought it was about time to display my adventurous side. I was sure I had an adventurous side... *surely I did.*

It was a beautiful Sunday morning. We would have to miss church to get to the meeting place on time. I didn't miss church often but this seemed to be one of those special occasions for which I could make an exception. I can remember thinking my priority that day was to find a pair of shorts to wear over my swimsuit because at my age the great cover-up was an art. I knew I would be the oldest person on this trip. I had at least 10 years on most of them. I really didn't want to look "un-cool."

When everyone else in our group was laughing and teasing, trying on helmets and life jackets, I was actually listening to the tour guide. I don't know, it seemed like the "respectful" thing to do and you know...what if there was an emergency of some kind, I should know how to save one of these crazy young people who didn't think it was necessary to listen. In just a few short minutes I soaked up a lot of information and gained a great deal of respect for the guide. He seemed knowledgeable. He said he had been down this river over 100 times. He sounded trustworthy to me!

As we approached the raft I scouted out what I thought would be the best seats for Mandy and me. She had been on several rafting trips all over the country. She was the one with experience but my 'mommy mode' was kicking in and I wanted us to be sensible and safe. It seemed reasonable to me that we should try to stay close to the tour guide. I wanted to hear his instructions, and I wanted us to be the first ones he would help in case of an emergency. It turned out to be a good choice, at least at first, because the people at the other end of the raft were responsible to push off shore and then jump into the raft. I wasn't sure I would have been agile enough to handle that little task, at least not gracefully. As it turned out I got to take my place, tuck my foot into the strap, get situated and watch the people at the other end push us off. Mandy was at my left and the guide was at the point of the raft, right behind us.

All was well until we actually got wet. It was late August but the water was freezing. There was no "getting used to it gradually." In the first two minutes we were soaked. We had no time to whine, however, because after the initial shock of cold we began to hear orders shouted out by our navigator, "Row left, row right!" I was a little slow on the uptake but soon fell into the rhythm. This wasn't just a joy ride. Each one of us had a job to do. There were a couple of short, calm stretches when I could actually just sit still, look around and enjoy God's beauty. During those moments I remember Mandy telling me to hang on and scoot in toward the center of the raft. She asked me over and over if I was okay. Okay? Of course I was okay, I was cool, I was spontaneous; look at me, I was actually participating in life, not just watching from the sidelines.

Roughly an hour into our trip we approached the

biggest drop of the entire course. We had been told about it, told what to do, how to do it, and I was ready. Despite our efforts to turn our raft slightly to the right, we hit the drop head on, causing the front to dive. That action in turn caused the back of the raft (the safest end by my earlier estimation) to shoot straight up in the air, out of the water. I don't remember what happened next, although later I would see a Kodak account of the whole ordeal because there were cameramen posted along the banks taking shots to sell to the rafters at the end of the tour.

My next conscious moment was the sensation of being propelled through the water at a high rate of speed. I couldn't see. I could hear only the rushing of the water. There was something heavy on top of me, holding me down, preventing me from rising to the surface. *Oh dear God...I'm under the raft.* I frantically began to flail and claw at the smooth, slick rubber on top of me. My arms were everywhere. I was trying to find something to grab hold of so I could stop. I needed to stop so the raft would get ahead of me. I needed to get my head up. Nothing I did made a difference. My body continued to rush down the river at the same speed as the raft and I couldn't get out from under it. I was completely trapped.

I had always heard that in times like this your life flashes before your eyes like a slide show. That didn't happen to me. I missed that particular slide show because I was too busy struggling. I was fighting like I'd never fought before. HOPE was happening. It wasn't something I consciously pulled to the forefront of my mind. It wasn't something I initiated or forced. HOPE automatically, instantly took over. *I will make it out of this...I won't die in this river...Please God, help me. Please God, help me.*

I don't know how or why, but my body shifted. I could label the happening by saying I probably hit a boulder, possibly my flailing limbs caught on some outcropping of brush or river bank at just the right moment to turn me. I'm sure I could come up with a hundred logical explanations, some coincidental event that just happened in the nick of time. I could tell it and claim it, even come to believe it as being just one of those "saved by the bell" kind of experiences. But why? Why would I want to explain it away or call it anything less than it was? I know without a shadow of a doubt, the force that turned my body that day was nothing short of miraculous. I cried out to God and he heard me.

Now I was floating sideways down the river instead of my previous feet-first fashion. Because my body shifted, I was able to raise my arms and push off the side of the raft. I was still floating under it, at the same speed, but now I could raise my head and clear my face at intervals and catch short snatches of breath. The sound of the rushing water was deafening. Now I was hearing something else though...it was my daughter; she was frantic. She was screaming, "My mom, my mom, my mom." Thank God. She hadn't fallen out; she was in the raft. Maybe others were as well. Someone would see me..someone would help me. *Thank you, Lord. Thank you!*

Later I found out I was the only one of my team in trouble. When we hit the drop, the guide had been thrown forward. His oar hit me square between the eyes and knocked me out—out of the boat and out of consciousness. I don't remember the impact or going into the water. The coldness of the water, the cold I had perceived as an imposition earlier, revived me, shocked me back into consciousness. The pictures show everyone was looking back for me but no one was looking in the area right around the raft. Then, captured in the shots you can see a head turn to the right. A young state trooper had spotted my bright pink helmet and thankfully he was quick to react. He reached down, took hold of my life jacket and pulled. I outweighed him by at least 20 pounds, but somehow, in one swift motion, I was back in the boat. *Thank you dear Lord, Thank you! Thank you!*

All the rafters wanted to stop and comfort me and I for sure needed comforting at that moment, but the raft was still moving and everyone had a job to do. The guide, now having regained his composure and his position at the point, was again barking out orders. I'm a total team player but I couldn't move. I just sat in the dead center of the raft. I was trying not to cry. I was trying harder to stop shaking, but my entire body was jerking violently. I coughed up river water for the next half hour. *Oh my dear Lord, I almost died down there...Oh my dear Lord.*

We were minutes from calm water and from our midway stop where a lunch break was to take place. I felt strange. I was stunned and confused. I felt I was having one of those "out of body" experiences you hear people talk about, watching everything around me from a distance, as if I weren't really there.

When the raft was pulled to shore, we were asked to get out and walk up the hill to where the lunch spread was waiting. Everyone gathered around my daughter and me. There were hugs. There were tears. Like a sheep, I blindly followed the other people in my group. Mandy was helping me and asking me question after question to check my responses. She suggested that we walk up to the resort and go to the restroom to wash the mascara off my face. I somehow made it up the path. We took my helmet off and began to wash my face only to find that it wasn't mascara but a bruise that ran from my hairline down to my lips.

I was battered, bruised and "knocked silly." I was so out of it I actually got back into the raft after lunch and finished the trip. By the end of the day I could barely move. The boulders and rocks in the river had beaten me up pretty badly. We bought the pictures the photographer had taken, as did many who were not even in our raft. To this day, looking at the pictures is difficult. I can hardly believe what I see.

I revisited that river often, in my mind and in my dreams. I talked to friends and family and found myself telling the story over and over again. I captivated my audiences with the amazing account of danger and rescue. I think talking about it helped me to deal with the trauma I had suffered. But more importantly it gave me the opportunity to give God the glory and talk about HOPE.

I learned that day that hope isn't just a butterfly emotion that drops in and impresses us on rare occasions. It isn't something that we observe and enjoy only to have it take flight and evade our grasp. Hope is a gift given to us by God; a gift that was meant to be un-wrapped, handled, and used throughout our lifetime. What a huge mistake it would be to underestimate its value...to re-wrap it and bury it in some bottom drawer, ever to be hidden and smothered by our doubt and unbelief. This gift of HOPE is our personal shield, our piece of armor. It upholds us in situations of grave danger; it shrouds and enfolds us even on the uneventful days. We must get acquainted with hope. We need HOPE...sometimes just to be able to get out of bed in the morning.

For me, this rafting rescue was the beginning of a series of rescues, a chain connecting one unbelievable event to another, a story of God at work in my insignificant, unworthy life. He, in his infinite mercy, has snatched us all from the grip of death time after time, most of which I'm sure we will never be aware of until we reach heaven's shore. I get chills when I hear stories of the 80 car pile-up that was missed because of lateness, a tragic plane crash, someone's scheduled flight, missed because of some incidental inconvenience, an injury that could have, should have paralyzed but miraculously did not.

I don't believe in coincidence. I believe in divine intervention. I know of six times in my life when I faced death head on; six times when I should have died, six times when God intervened and spared my life. I would like to share these incredible stories of hope and faith. I would like to talk about God Almighty, the King of Kings, and Lord of Lords, who has answered prayer, saved my life, and proved Himself to me over and over again. Together, let's focus on God's power, His mercy, His perfect timing, His incredible love and then together, let's give Him glory.

A Little Deeper

In I Samuel 17:37 we read, "The Lord who delivered me from the paw of the lion and the paw of the bear will deliver me from the hand of this Philistine."

This emphatic affirmation was declared by a young boy with such conviction and passion it convinced a King to step outside the line of logic, outside the soundness of wartime strategy. Moved by David's resolve, King Saul agreed to let a mere boy go into battle against a giant. David's age and size, his plan and his weapons didn't meet with battle standards, but in the long run all he really needed was his belief and faith in God Almighty.

God's divine will, His power, His intervention won the victory. Throughout his lifetime, David gives praise over and over again for God's deliverance. Read:

Psalm 86:13
Psalm 107:6
Psalm 116:8

I expected that sitting by the tour guide on this rafting trip I was placing my daughter and myself in the best possible position. I expected that because we were near him we'd be safe. Actually, I put my trust in the source that proved to be the greatest threat.

I'm a die-hard control freak. It's taken me most of my life to learn that despite my planning, life sometimes takes its own direction. What a comfort to know God is always in tune. Nothing sneaks up on Him. He is all knowing, ever caring. He is absolute. He is never changing. He's always in control. When that lesson is learned and lived out it brings sweet relief. I Praise God for His deliverance. I give Him glory for his intervention.

"I praise You Awesome God for Your love and Your care. I praise You for watching over me and protecting me. I know You reached down from on high and took hold of me…I know You drew me out of those deep waters. (Ps 18:16) I know You spared my life. I love You. I thank You and I praise You!"

TWO

THE EARLY YEARS

"Those who know your name will trust in you,
for you, Lord, have never forsaken
those who seek you." Psalm 9:10

Growing up I was sandwiched between two perfect, talented and beautiful, over achievers. My sister is six years older than I. Her special gifts are patience, determination, and laughter. She loves to laugh and is a master at making others laugh as well. Her sense of humor is infectious. Living in the shadow of this pretty, petite, energetic beauty was intimidating. Diann was the stuff cheerleaders were made of and I spent much of my awkward years being crazy jealous of her. During all the years growing up as children, when we were not close because of our age difference, we've more than made up for as adults. She's my sister by chance but truly my friend by choice. My brother, Boyd, was the golden child. He's 8 years younger than I, and you do the math, 14 years younger than my sister. About the time mom and dad figured two girls would be their forever family, here comes the "boy" child, the one who would carry on the family name. Yeah, more often than not I was jealous of him too. He was an absolutely gorgeous child and grew up without misplacing any of those gorgeous genes. What a head turner...he is smart, witty, charming and hardworking. We're extremely close as adults. I admire and love him very much.

So, as the proverbial "middle child" here, I'm doing my best to wring out a bit of sympathy. We middle kids get a raw deal. We never quite measure up to the first-born and we're just not cute enough to compete with the baby. Poor "middle kids" of the world! Okay...I'm exaggerating....truthfully, I'm not sure if that "middle child" thing is real or if it's just an excuse to use when we middle children don't measure up to our own expectations. I only know that for most of my growing up years I felt "less than." I was chubby and freckled faced. I didn't seem to fit. I came to grips with the fact that there was nothing special about me and that things would never come easy for me. That realization became a relentless, sometimes ruthless driving force that has propelled me throughout my entire life. So, I wasn't special, nothing would come easy...I would just have to try harder.

One important thing that did come to me as a birth right, however, and the thing I value above all is that I was born into a Christian home. My parents were believers. They both knew Jesus Christ as their Lord and Savior. They took us to Sunday School and Church. We read the Bible in our home. As a result, I accepted the Lord as my Savior when I was 9 years old. A school mate had done a wonderful job witnessing to me and soon after I asked my Dad to walk me down the aisle of an old Southern Baptist Church during an altar call. Of all the memories I have tucked away, some happy, some sad, none can compare to the day I gave my heart to the Lord and accepted His amazing gift of salvation. He had been gently calling me...persistently knocking at my heart's door. Ours has been a constant, real, and abiding relationship. He became my Redeemer, Savior, and Friend. He has loved me, lead me, chastened me, rejoiced with me, and comforted me. He has seen fit to hold me, hedge me about, protect me, and save my life countless times. How fortunate I was to be born into a family of believers. How blessed I was to be born into the family of God.

For the most part, I'm sure I was a pretty normal kid. I played hard, laughed a lot, and dreamed big. There was really only one slightly abnormal thing about my growing up years that set me apart from my sister and brother and set me apart from the other kids as well, I guess. I can remember having what my parents called "spells." I would get lightheaded, short of breath, weak, and felt as though I was going to pass out. At that point in time, these little spells were only bothersome. They didn't happen too often, probably only five or six times a year and because it wasn't an ongoing and consistent problem we didn't see a physician about it. Believe it or not, back in those dark ages kids didn't see a doctor that often. You might go if there was a fever involved or if your injury was bad enough that all the normal home remedies failed to stop the bleeding. (It's a wonder there are so many of us baby boomers around. How on earth did we survive without all the rules and restraints, the special diets, the safety equipment?)

The years rushed by. I worked twenty to thirty hours a week all through my junior and senior year of high school and that part time job melded into a full-time position the day after graduation.

I was married at 18 and just before my 20th birthday my first child was born. During those prenatal visits to the doctor's office, I was told I had a slight heart murmur. Even though I was experiencing more and more of these "spells," I brushed it off and truly didn't worry. I was told it was minor, so I mentally made the move to major on the major (God, family, job, finances) and minor on the minor.

Less than two years later I was at the doctor's office again complaining of flu like symptoms that had lasted for more than two weeks. He asked me if I could be pregnant. I told him, "Oh no, I'm sure I'm not pregnant." He said we should probably do a test just in case. The test results marked a giant milestone in my life, a point in time when I learned "never to say never." Sure enough, I was expecting, and as soon as I knew the answer for my feeling so ill, I was better. Better, except for those troublesome times when I experienced the shortness of breath, the weakness, the barely hanging on to consciousness. On one of my prenatal visits, my new doctor asked if I had ever noticed any abnormalities in my heart rhythm. I told him I had a heart murmur and he said, "No, I don't believe it's a murmur...it's an arrhythmia." There it was...my introduction to a lifelong ailment that I've struggled with to this very day.

Several years and two babies later I found myself in the doctor's office again, this time "knowing" I was probably pregnant. I was just looking for professional confirmation. By this point in my life I was doing the egg shell walk, never knowing when I was going to have an arrhythmia episode and living in fear that another one could be just around the corner. I had graduated from several episodes a year to at least three or four a month. The events were debilitating. The fear paralyzed me. I was a working mom. Having two boys, two years apart, a husband, a home to run, and a full-time job, there was no time to pamper myself because of a heart that didn't always keep a regular beat. During one particular visit to my family doctor, he scolded me, saying it had been quite some time since he had seen me. I told him I thought I was expecting another child. He explained that I should have been back periodically to keep an eye on the arrhythmia. Somehow I had missed those instructions and had just been suffering in silence for seven years. I was extremely regimented about taking my two boys to the pediatrician, but in my busy-ness and ignorance, I had failed to exercise caution about my own health. (Dear busy moms of the world, I hope you didn't miss it...there was a subtle, loving reminder flying off the page just for you.)

During this visit he gave my ailment a name. He no longer referred to it as an arrhythmia...he called it by it's own name...Atrial Fibrillation. It was as if he had said, "Nancy, I'd like for you to meet A-Fib. You two will become very, very close. A-Fib will be your most faithful companion; he'll stick close by your side. He'll be your personal cross to bear, the literal thorn in your side, a heavy weight around your neck, and the reason for count-less heartaches and unfulfilled dreams."

Believe it or not, it was 1976 and he spoke with me about ending the pregnancy. In his opinion, carrying this child was going to prove to be an enormous challenge. He said it was likely I would spend most of it in bed. He warned my heart might not be able to withstand the strain of childbirth. As I listened, I was doing what I had trained myself to do... I searched for the positive. I grabbed on to the "could cause" and the "might prove to be" phrases he used and translated them into the language of HOPE. Instantly, I chose to believe that somehow, someway, God would see me through this pregnancy. Although my Doctor couldn't put me on an arrhythmia medication during pregnancy, he would do so as soon as the baby was born. In my mind and in my heart there was a calming presence telling me that it would be okay...everything would be okay. I had been raising my children, working full time, handling all the cooking, cleaning, laundry, and shopping. I had been teaching Sunday School, singing in the Church choir, and maintaining close friendships, all without the medication. I could add pregnancy to the mix; I just knew I could. Even though I greatly respected my physician's medical expertise and knew that he had only my best interest in mind, I had, on a much more consistent basis, been visiting the "Great Physician." I believed with all my heart that HE had a plan for my life and for the life of this child.

I wrapped the hard, cold facts in a giant shell of HOPE and I left his office ready to battle whatever enemy I might have to face in the next few months. At that time I didn't share with my husband, friends, or family what I had learned about my physical situation. Looking back, I was probably trying to minimize it in my own mind. I didn't want anyone to pity me or treat me differently. I also didn't want to burden anyone. Most of all, I didn't want to become one of those people who constantly talk about their illness and how bad they feel. I didn't want to appear self-absorbed, self-consumed. I didn't want to be perceived as being weak. A-N-D, okay, I guess if I talked about it at length with family and friends, it would mean that I would have to deal with it up close and personal. I just needed to leave it buried for the time being. I know now that I was going through a denial of sorts. I think it was a case of self preservation. Of course, I shared the good news of the baby on the way. That was my focus...the baby. I continued to handle all my responsibilities just as I had been doing up to that point. One day at a time................

A Little Deeper

Think of a time in your life when you received really bad news. How did you react? How did you deal with it?

In the beginning, my way of 'dealing' was to shelf the subject in a sort of go-on-in-spite-of-it fashion. That kind of grit-your-teeth, self-reliant attitude only initiates a vicious circle of growing problems that feed on one another.

Psalm 55:22 says, "Cast your cares on the Lord and He will sustain you." Webster lays out the tell-all definition of the word 'cast' with the first offering. The word cast means 'to cause to move or send forth by throwing.' God was waiting for me, longing to take my burden of bad news and carry it for me. But in order for Him to carry it, I had to let it go. He didn't pry it from my arms. He didn't force me to turn it loose. The "letting go" was my part of the deal.

I know I wasted time trying to understand why this calamity wore my name tag. In the Old Testament, Job's friends preached to him that he needed to try to 'understand' his suffering so that he could better deal with it. I learned it wasn't really important to understand. I will never understand half the things that happen in this world. My job is to trust....simply let go and trust.

Read:

Isaiah 49:13
Psalm 56:3-4
Proverbs 3:5

Trusting in the midst of the storm often means that we are taking a less than proactive approach. It's in our makeup to want to 'do something', and yet God tells us to "be still and know that He is God." (Psalm 46:10)

I was struggling in an airport one day, pulling and puffing, barely managing the weight of my packed bags. Convinced that I could 'handle' this load, I forged ahead. When I finally reached the line to check my luggage, I turned around just in time to see an airport attendant rolling a cart loaded with only two bags. Unlike me, the woman walking beside him wasn't out of breath or disheveled in the least. The gentleman spoke up to tell me, "I was going to help you. There was plenty of room on the cart for your things. But you never slowed down long enough to let me load your bags...."

"Oh, Lord, when the bad news comes, when the burden is too great, teach me to slow down...help me to willingly, immediately give up my load ...cast my burdens and my cares on You, trusting that You will indeed sustain me."

THREE

AGAINST ALL ODDS

*"Do not be afraid. Stand firm and you will see
the deliverance the Lord will bring you today.
The Lord will fight for you: you need only to be still."*
Exodus 14: 13, 14

I learned that keeping my blood pressure down was of utmost concern. If my blood pressure went up, it increased the likelihood of an A-Fib episode. And if my pressure rose too far beyond a normal range I would have to be put on bed rest. I probably needed bed rest... certainly I had been burning the candle at both ends, rushing, stretching, scheduling, trying to cover all the bases. But bed rest just wasn't an option. There was no way I could do that. *Please God, keep me strong.* I had always worked and we had come to depend on my income to meet our financial obligations. Who would help me with the boys; what about the cooking, the cleaning, the shopping, the laundry? I would just have to stay well. I opened my eyes each day praying that God would give me strength...praying that HE would help me to manage and keep me well.

When we come to the end of ourselves and realize

how truly dependent we are on God, that without Him we are nothing, we can do nothing- that's actually the best place to be. Only then do we find the absolute passion to live close to Him every minute of the day. It keeps us humble. It keeps us on our knees. Like a child, we hold His hand tighter and tighter because we know that crossing this particular street in life is dangerous. The cars are rushing by, the horns are blaring, and the opposite corner seems like an eternity away. God whispers in our ear, "Hold my hand, don't let go." We move forward, our steps in sync with the Master, our hand gripping tightly to His. We don't rush ahead. We're careful not to lag behind. These are truly the best times in our journey with God. These are the sweetest moments because during these times we get over ourselves and know that, beyond a doubt, without Him this crossing would be impossible.

I take comfort in David's journals. In Psalm 142, we find him crying out to God. He recognizes his need. He admits that he's desperate and he begs for God to hear him. Verse 7 says, "Set me free from my prison that I may praise your name." David was asking God to protect him through the perilous days when King Saul hunted him incessantly, intending to kill him. Verse 4 says, "Look to my right and see; no one is concerned for me." A King was accustomed to having an armed guard at his right at all times, there to protect and defend him. But here's David, hiding out in a cold, dark cave, fearing for his life; he's alone and afraid. He began this chapter with the words, "I cry aloud to the Lord."

During these crucial days of pregnancy, as I carried this precious child, I too cried aloud to the Lord. I felt alone and afraid. All the odds seemed to be stacked up against me. I was desperate.

Psalm 121 begins by saying, "I lift my eyes to the hills- where does my help come from? My help comes from the Lord, the Maker of heaven and earth." Verse 3 of that chapter follows with confirmation that God indeed sees our need; He answers our prayer. "He will not let your foot slip- He who watches over you will not slumber." Praise God for answered prayer. Much to my doctor's surprise, I was able to keep up with my schedule until the very last days of my pregnancy. Three weeks before my due date, I did have to quit working and was told to conform to strict bed rest. I did what any sane mother-to-be should do...I called my mom. Even though she and my dad were out of town on one of their RV trips, they came to my rescue. Mom stepped in to take care of me and EVERYTHING else. I don't know...call me crazy, but I was tentative to ask for help; I was embarrassed to need the help and I hated having to be taken care of. I was dreading the next three weeks, not because I wasn't enjoying having my mother with me, but because I felt like it was an imposition for her.

Well, let me say again...praise God for answered prayer. Mom had only been there three days (not weeks) and on the third night my water broke. Wow...it was happening...I had made it...my baby was on the way. "She" was beautiful by the way. Not only was the gender different...her red hair and blue eyes were a delightful surprise.

By this time, my ever-faithful buddy, A-Fib, was elbowing his way through the crowd, vying for a more front-of-the-line position in my life. Having beat the odds, not only of completing the pregnancy, but handling the stress of labor and childbirth, now my doctor and I joined forces to find a medication that would at least help curb the increasing number of episodes I was having. There were many options, but even more side effects. This was a fearful and fragile balancing act.

After my daughter was born, I wasn't able to go back to work at the stock brokerage where I had been for several years. I tried to limit some stress by working part time as a church secretary during the hours that Michael and Matthew were in school. I was able to take Mandy with me. I babysat some as well. Although both part time jobs enabled me to contribute at least some income, the shift away from the better, full-time job ended up putting quite a strain on our total household finances. My husband's job was very erratic. He worked construction, so when the weather interrupted his work, it also interrupted our income. Much of my memory of those years revolves around how I hated rain and snow. Each month proved to be an exercise of the "RP to PP shuffle." The dance of "Robbing Peter to Pay Paul" was truly an art and each new month found me enrolled for yet another two-step class. My first priority was the house payment, but everything else was shuffled and re-arranged so that we just barely made it each month. In those days we didn't have caller ID so there were many anxious moments when answering the phone because most of the time it was someone demanding payment.

Only months into this new working situation our finances were in big trouble, and so was our marriage. My husband and I had always been red hot lovers, but never good friends. Because there was no friendship and no feeling of equitable input or partnership, we had nothing that even resembled a unified front. The enemies we faced found it easy to break through our lines. The strongest skirmish we could muster was stymied at the get-go because my husband's weapons were anger and intimidation and I countered with silence.

I praise God that despite the constant and painful turmoil, I was fervent in keeping my focus on the children. I was diligent about not missing anything in their lives. I was attentive and involved. I'm so thankful that I didn't let our failing finances, our failing marriage, or my failing health steal the joy of those precious years. I believe that to a great extent focus is a choice. We determine our priorities. I praise God for "upholding me with His mighty right hand." (Isaiah 41:10) As I look back to those years...I do remember the hard times...they just aren't the first thing I remember. I am blessed instead with memories of laughter, birthday parties, lunch boxes, homework, report cards, singing, piano playing, games, make believe, Vacation Bible School, and sports. Thank You, Lord, for the sweet, sweet memories. I continued to cry to the Lord. And God continued to uphold me. He was the only Hope in my life. I treasured and held closely the words of Psalm 130:5, I wait for the Lord, my soul waits, and in His word I put my hope."

A Little Deeper

Have there been times in your life when you staged a battle; a seemingly 'no-win' situation? Reassess the time that comes to mind first. What was your first reaction? How did you handle the fear? What was the outcome?

How did it affect your faith? How did it affect your walk with God?

We find recorded in Exodus 14, the story of the Israelites as they ran from Egypt. They looked up, in verse 10, and saw the Egyptians in hot pursuit. As Pharaoh's soldiers closed in, their fear mounted. They lashed out at Moses, blaming him for the seemingly hopeless situation. Moses answered the cries of the people in verse 13 and 14, "Do not be afraid. Stand firm and you will see the deliverance the Lord will bring you today.... The Lord will fight for you...." We know the end of the story. God parted the Red Sea, allowing the Israelites to walk across on dry ground. The best part of the story is that through the trials, through the hardship and fear, the people of Israel learned to trust God. Verse 31 says, "And when the Israelites saw the great power the Lord displayed against the Egyptians, the people feared the Lord and put their trust in him..."

Can you close your eyes and visualize God fighting for you when you face the battles in your life?

"Oh, Lord, help me to remember when the fear closes in that You are fighting for me. Thank You for the promise that You will never leave me. Teach me courage based on Your strength and power. Increase my faith. I put my trust in You."

FOUR

SOMETHING'S GOTTA CHANGE

"Shout for joy, O heavens; rejoice,
O earth; burst into song, O mountains!
For the Lord comforts his people and will have
compassion on his afflicted ones," Isaiah 49:13

My daughter was four years old when my cardiologist put me on yet another new medication. Each would work for a while and then become ineffective. I would advance to the next rung on the ladder, hoping that this 'new one' would keep my heart behaving for a period of time. My track record wasn't panning out well. It seemed I could expect only about 6 months of reprieve and then we would need to change tactics, change medication. The cycle was discouraging. But it kept me seeking God for answers and help. It kept me in a holding pattern...holding on to HOPE.

1984 proved to be a trying year. Michael was 16 years old...Matt was 14 and Mandy was 7. Not only had finances crumbled, our marriage was crumbling as well. We were hanging on for the sake of our children. We were hanging on for the sake of our parents. We went through the motions but we were growing apart at a runaway speed. The love and affection had been replaced with anger, doubt, suspicion, and insecurity. I was totally disillusioned. This isn't what I had expected and I was angry...angry at destiny, angry at the cards of life dealt to me, and perhaps even angry at God.

In the winter of that year I made an appointment with my family doctor to address my health issues. He changed my medication and coupled it with a blood thinner. I was told that my Atrial Fibrillation had progressed to dangerous levels; dangerous because I was flopping back and forth between a sinus rhythm and erratic rhythm so often there was probability of forming a blood clot resulting in a stroke. I was only 36 years old and facing the fact that this ordeal had stretched beyond dealing with the episodes affecting the quality of my life...I could actually have a stroke or a heart attack. I could die. I was advised to avoid stressful situations, exercise, eat healthy meals, take my medications and have regular protime lab tests to keep tabs on the effects of the blood thinner.

I remember a "mini" breakdown of sorts. It's the hardest thing in the world to process the facts that all point to the negative. I questioned whether I could handle this new information along with the marriage and financial issues I was already dealing with. I retreated...not to a beach, a villa, or even a spa...I just escaped to a far away place inside myself. When you're a mom you have to show up at meal time, at car pool time, and on laundry and grocery shopping day. But during the next few weeks my body showed up alone. My spirit, my thoughts, and my emotions, that part of me deep inside where nobody sees, was in another place. I prayed and I cried. I recognized the darkness and the depression that was overpowering me, but alone I couldn't fight the demons. I pleaded with God to lift me up and out of the blackness. Psalm 18:28 says, "You, O lord, keep my lamp burning; my God turns my darkness into light." I claimed that verse and others like it and God in His mercy lifted me into the light.

With His help I began to pull the bits and pieces of myself back together again. With His help, a little at a time, I was able to find control and begin to cope. I analyzed the stressful components in my life and determined to do whatever necessary to make things better.

First of all I came clean with my family and friends about the heart problem and the medication I was taking. The next thing I addressed was our finances. We were digging the hole deeper and deeper as each month rolled by. The wider the gap became between our income and our obligations, the wider the chasm grew that separated my husband and I. We desperately needed a healthy second income, something we could count on, come rain or shine. Armed with that reality, I began to look for full-time work. I surmised that working a full-time job, even saddled with health problems, would be less stressful than worrying about the bills month after month. I suppose at the time I agreed with the reasoning of Washington Irving when years ago he wrote,

"There is a certain relief in change, even though it be from bad to worse! As I have often found in traveling in a stagecoach, it is sometimes a comfort to shift one's position, and be bruised in a new place."

I couldn't bear the present strain any longer. The choice to go to work full time was probably just a shift in position and more than likely would only leave me bruised in a new place, but I had to do something.

One definition of stupidity is to keep doing what you're doing and expect different results. Andy Warhol said it this way, "They say that time changes things, but you actually have to change them yourself." I was petrified of losing our home. Our car payment was getting made just ahead of the repo man every month. Somebody needed to take action. I was the only somebody I had influence over so I flew into motion.

Was I letting God be in control of my life or was I taking control from Him? Did I seek his wisdom intently enough? Was I working or was God working through me? I still am not sure of answers to these questions. But I do know now, that throughout my life, God has used the worst of circumstances to teach me the most and this was definitely a time of learning. Hope labeled the pages in the book of these days and months and years with the darkest of indelible markers. Even on those occasions when the book was misplaced in the maze of other confusing and all-consuming books, I was always able to find it again, tuck it under my arm and march on.

It didn't take me long to find a job. I had references, a ton of training, great work ethic and superb skills. In March of 1985, I went to work at a retail automobile business. I can remember thinking the pay was okay; it was 10 minutes from my house; I could run home for lunch.

It wasn't as if I went back to full time work screaming and kicking. I was looking forward to relieving the financial tension. In all honesty, however, I harbored some bitterness that my husband's choice of jobs resulted in 3-4 months of missed work a year. The seasonal aspects of construction made it extremely hard on our family. I wanted things to be better. I so wanted things to be better.

In the meantime I struggled with A-Fib. By the late 1980's I was admitted to the hospital several times a year. Most of the time I could muddle through at work or at home and it would pass, but more and more frequently, I needed to get help. It became routine that I would go into the Emergency Room and the ER doctors would hook me up to intravenous medications in order to bring me back into sinus rhythm.

I was made aware that even though Atrial Fibrillation is not rare, the fact that we were having such a hard time finding a medication that would control it was quite unusual. It was always a surprise to me, as well as the doctors, that time after time I would break through one prescription and need to move on to a new one.

The road traveled the next few years was rocky. Juggling job, home, church, husband, and children left little time for the important questions. I don't believe I stopped long enough to ask if my motives were pure or if God was pleased with my heart. I remember giving Him what was left over of me at the end of a day, but never the first fruits of my time.

During those years of struggle, my children filled the gaps, the places that would have been otherwise so void if not for them. They were my inspiration, my joy, and my anchor. They kept my life in focus and made it all seem worth while. They were a positive, consistent source of my strength and passion. What joy they've brought me over the years.

We did finally get a handle on our finances. I was making a respectable income...nothing special, but enough to change our overall picture. It was a struggle, however. I was paying for the opportunity of working full time. The medicines offered only limited help. They failed to keep all the episodes at bay.

A Little Deeper

Think of a time in your life when you summarized your situation and knew that something must change. Maybe it was physical, financial, emotional, spiritual, or moral. Did you consult God? Did you seek His leading?

How do you handle your fears that center around unknown change?

The book of Ruth tells a beautiful story of a woman going through what was more than likely unanticipated and certainly unwelcome change. Ruth found herself in the midst of the worst kind of turmoil. Her husband died leaving her destitute and in a land of great famine. At a time in her life when she was grieving and lonely, in painful despair and chaos, Ruth makes the most important decision of her life. She tells her widowed mother-in-law in Ruth 1:16-18 that she has decided to turn from the pagan Gods of her homeland, Moab. She has decided to follow the true and living God. She swears an allegiance not only to God Jehovah but to Naomi as well.

Both women, recently widowed, alone, afraid, and hungry, step out in desperation to effect change. Because they had heard there was food enough in Bethlehem, they packed up and moved across country. Talk about upheaval. Talk about disruption. Once in Bethlehem, Ruth was forced to go to work. I feel sure her heart's desire would have been to be a wife, a mother, a homemaker. But that wasn't her reality. She found herself instead, in a position of caretaker and provider. Out of that necessity she went to work gleaning what was left in the barley fields after the harvesters had passed through. Where did Ruth find that kind of strength in that kind of tumult? I think we have to go back to verse 16 again when she speaks those now famous words to Naomi, "your people will be my people and your God my God." There, indeed, is the answer...there, indeed, is the source of Ruth's strength and courage in the midst of change. She was able to step out into the unknown because God supplied the strength for the journey. Ruth was rewarded for her loyalty to Naomi and her faithfulness to God. She was rewarded for her willingness.

Boaz, the owner of the fields, and her kinsman redeemer, spotted her, was drawn to her and married her. They had a son named Obed... who was the father of Jesse... who was the father of David.

"Oh, Lord, You are my strength and my shield. I pray for Your help especially when life seems unstable. Help me when the familiar is snatched away. Give me courage when dealing with change. When I am on new and shaky ground, be my foundation and my cornerstone. Bless me indeed, I pray!"

FIVE

MONEY MOTIVATED

"When I came to the spring today, I said,
'O Lord, God of my master Abraham,
if you will, please grant success to the journey
on which I have come." Genesis 24:42

It was such a relief to be able to make ends meet, but I knew if we had any sort of emergency, big or small, it would throw us right back into our previous rut. I wanted a savings account. I wanted the security of a nest egg, a safety net, a reserve to fall back on. At this point in time we were holding the bill collectors at bay and most of our finances were being handled in a somewhat "on-time" fashion. I was grateful for the progress, but knew living in the "check-to-check," "month-to-month" zone was dangerous. I was having trouble finding my balance on the "budget bridge of life" and unless I beat that wicked troll once and for all I would have to deal with him over and over again. I was running from a monster and my fear wouldn't allow me to slow down to catch my breath. I knew how close we had been to losing everything and I was determined to run as fast as necessary to defeat this foe that threatened me and my family.

Sure, I know what you're thinking...I traded stress for stress, but somehow this load seemed lighter... better...at least more under my control. Actually, not being 3 and 4 months behind on the bills felt so good I even considered working two jobs. If making decent money made this kind of difference...maybe making more money would be the waving of the wand that could turn my life into the story-book promise I had dreamed it would be.

There were so many issues though. The state of my marriage and the absence of a meaningful relationship with my husband was a constant lump in my throat and hole in my heart. Our financial situation was daunting. My boys were teenagers now and beginning to question the contra-diction between the values we talked and the reality we walked. And then, of course, always present and unrelent-ing, my health issues continued to occupy that front row seat in my life. By nature I'm a fixer, but the more I band-aided a problem, the deeper the wound spread. I was desperate. I felt so alone... "me against the world." I finally stumbled onto something that felt good....felt right. I liked this new prescription...this miracle drug of money and I plugged it in to every problem I could see, believing it would cure all the diseases that plagued my life.

A line from the movie, John Q, comes to mind. Trapped in a no-win situation, without the money or health insurance to cover a heart transplant for his young son, Denzel Washington's character was planning to take his own life in order to give his son the heart he so desperately needed to live. The scene finds the father standing at the bedside of his critically ill son. He was saying goodbye. His advice included, "Be a man of your word, son; if you say something, do it. Treat the girls like the princesses they are..." Then, somewhere meshed in with all the crucial things he had chosen to say to his son, he said, "Make choices that allow you to earn a lot of money, life is easier with money." That statement, in a nutshell became my waving flag. Yea...Surely life would be easier with money....

I believe the major driving force inside me at this point in time was survival. I know I prayed hard and long about all the issues that were defeating me and my family. But when there seemed to be no help...no change on the horizon, I stepped out and took things into my own hands. I forced change. Sometimes God leads us to step out of our comfort zone and effect change. I can't tell you if the direction I took was, indeed, God's plan for me at the time. It's certainly possible that I came up with my own plan and then asked God to bless it. But one thing I do know...one thing I'm sure of is that no matter where we go...no matter what we do, God is there. He never leaves us nor forsakes us. (Deut. 31:8) He uses the pain we feel, the heartache we endure, our victories, our defeats. He uses them all to mold us and shape us into the vessel He can use in the future if we will let Him.

After working within the dealership for almost a year, I was anxious for advancement. I decided to start applying for every position that opened up, at least every position I considered to be a promotion. I worked as an Administrative Assistant; I worked in the Service Department; I worked as a Title Clerk, and finally as an assistant in the Financial Department. After stepping in to help with payroll at one point, I got a glimpse of the income levels for every job description within the organization. From the technicians in the shop to the parts counter people to the salespeople, to the Financial Service Coordinators to the Sales Managers to the General Manager, I saw it all. What an eye opener!

If it was possible for these people to do so well financially, it was possible for me. This was back in the 1980s, however, and as a general rule there weren't many women on the sales staff, few women in the service or parts departments and women certainly didn't occupy significant managerial positions within a retail automobile business. Being a female and aiming for that particular brass ring was unheard of. Even so, I began my campaign to reach for the stars.

My first real opportunity came when I overheard the Financial Service Director talking about the need to use the follow-up program that was included in our last software update. The problem was that no one in the department had time to learn it, work with it, test it, and get it up and running. SO....at night I began taking the instruction manual home and I studied, studied, studied. I came in early as often as I could and tested out all the things I had been learning. After I was sure of myself, I volunteered to help out. I printed off the previous month's business, printed off individual letters, reports and graphs. I was proud of the results and luckily my efforts got some attention. Looking back I think everyone saw me as some kind of computer guru. They didn't know how long I had been cramming for that particular exam.

That initiative earned an opportunity for me to work as a back up person in the Finance Department during particularly busy times. It was excellent training for something that was on the horizon...something I didn't have a clue was just around the corner....

I kept my eyes and ears open. I was considered for every opening that came up. At least I was led to believe I was being considered. But after four promotions and four years later my advancing through the ranks seemed to come to a halt. I wondered if I was being passed up because I was a woman. Perhaps the owners didn't recognize my drive and my tenacious personality. I wondered if I had gotten 'pigeon holed'. Did my bosses only see me in light of what I was handling at the present time? Were they reluctant to move me because they were happy with the job I was doing where I was?

I was discouraged and started to believe that I had capped out. Maybe I had gone as far up as I would be allowed to go within this company. I was impatient and disenchanted with my job. I started putting out feelers, looking for jobs within other organizations.

One afternoon the General Manager initiated a conversation with me. It felt a little strange. Out of the blue he was asking me how I was, how my family was. Normally he didn't have much time for chit chat, so I found his interest surprising...maybe even hopeful. He set up a sort of loose appointment with me and told me he would like to visit with me about something when I had a minute. My goodness! He could have just paged me to his office. He was the boss, after all.

Nevertheless, we made an appointment. When the day rolled around for us to meet, he was tied up elsewhere and we rescheduled. It ended up we had to reschedule several times, so by the time we actually connected, I was still curious but had decided the reason for our meeting must not be anything too exciting or important.

I knocked on the open door and was asked to step

and close the door behind me. *(Oh, a closed-door meeting! Had someone mistaken my impatience for a bad attitude? Had someone found out I was applying for jobs outside the company? Was I in trouble?)* I just wanted a better job, more money. I didn't want to lose the job I had. "Nancy, have a seat. I'm sorry we've had such a hard time making this meeting happen."

"Oh, that's all right, don't worry about it," I rushed to get a cheerful word in edgewise. For some reason I had the feeling I was in trouble and I thought my best defense was to at least be cheerful.

"Nancy, I saw Bob at the Charcoal Broiler a couple of weeks ago" *(Oh, man, just what I thought. I was in trouble. I recently sent Bob a resume)* and I hope you'll forgive us for talking about you, but he said you were asking about a job within the stock brokerage firm." I was about to butt in and defend myself, but he wasn't finished, so I simply met his eyes and nodded. "Nancy, I just want you to know we're really happy with your accomplishments here. You've done a tremendous job over the last four years. I know you've been applying for a full-time position in the Financial Service Department and I think you're probably disappointed that we decided to hire someone else." (I wasn't just disappointed, I was down right angry. Not only had they hired someone from outside the company, they actually asked me to train him. Talk about adding insult to injury!) "I recognize how ambitious you are and I just want you to know I'd sure hate to see you leave us right now." *Whoa! He was taking me through quite a range of emotions here.*

"Well, yes, I was disappointed. I felt like you passed me up a couple of times, first for the Office Manager spot and then the Finance Department." *(He opened up this can of worms...might as well talk about it.)* "I am ambitious. I feel like I'm ready to move forward. I've learned a lot. I've grown a lot. My fear is that you only see me in a clerical position and I'll never get the chance to prove what I'm really capable of." Now he was staring me down. Our eyes were locked and it seemed like some kind of stand-off. I conjured up the idea that the first one to look away would lose; I don't know what, just lose somehow. Looking back I know the conflict was of my own making. I felt like a 'B' string player being pulled off the bench and thrown into the game. I had been waiting for my shot, my chance to prove myself. I could run offense AND defense. Sitting there on that bench I had a front row view of the game. I had learned the plays, the moves, the strategy, and I had resolved I could do it all. I just wanted the chance to run.

As it turned out I was defending ground that wasn't even at stake. I was trying way too hard to be frank, be tough, and assertive, when in actuality the situation really didn't call for that sort of approach.

He blinked. I'm sure he blinked, so I backed off and relaxed a little. In my mind I had won that round. "You are absolutely right!" His statement was firm and emphatic. *Okay...I knew I was right...but..about what specifically?* The silence that followed was deafening. I had heard that in negotiations the first one to speak was the loser. I'm not sure why I perceived we were negotiating, but, man, I sure didn't want to lose. He waited for me to voice the question rolling around in my head. When I didn't, he continued, "What I mean is that I agree. You HAVE learned a lot. You've grown a lot and I think you've proven to us that you're ready to move forward. That's why I would sure hate to see you leave us to take another job right now. There's something big on the horizon and I think it would be a perfect fit for you." *(Whoa...this was actually going my way...this sounded a little like good news!)*

"Is someone leaving?"

"No, not that I'm aware of anyway. I apologize upfront for being vague and I need to insist that our conversation be kept in strict confidence."

"Of course," I complied. "What's going on?"

He lowered his head and his voice. *Wow, what was I about to hear?* "Can I just tell you for now that we're looking into a new car line, a brand new line, and long story short, I'm just trying to encourage you to hang on until this thing unfolds. I really think it will be in your best interest."

"Are you talking about a new car company?"

"Yes." I read volumes in his one-word answer.

"Seems like you're excited about it?" Now I was fishing.

"Yeah, I'm excited; it's gonna be a big deal."

Again there was silence and I could tell he had gone as far as he was going to go. I was flattered that he had shared as much as he had. "Well, that's enough for me," I said. "If you're excited, I'm excited. You bet I'll hang on. I just need to make some real money and if you see that in the picture for me, I can definitely hang on." We spoke again briefly about the importance of keeping our conversation confidential and he told me he would get back to me as soon as he was able.

It seemed forever before I heard anything more, but actually it was probably only a couple of months before the secret started to leak. *"A different kind of car...A different kind of company."* The motto for the new car company rang in my ears. The more I heard the more I wanted to hear. I did my homework. I prayed. I waited. Finally, an offer was made. In the fall of 1990 I was given the opportunity to be part of a 5 person team to open up a brand new SATURN facility. I took on being the Office Manager/ Finance Manager.

Though expectations were initially modest and salary arrangements were limited, it was a good boost for me. I probably doubled what I had been making and it would make things better for me and my family. I had definitely become very motivated, aggressive, and ambitious. I saw this as my opportunity and I was determined to make the most of it.

The car line as a whole got off to an amazing start. Ours was the first Saturn store in Colorado. Under the leadership of a new, visionary General Manager, our little store that had originally projected 30 new car sales a month, began the second year of business averaging between 80 and 100 sales per month. Life was good. Soon I was able to hire an Office Manager and move into the Finance Office full time. This was my first commission based position. Going from an hourly situation to a commission basis presents too much uncertainty for many people. There were times I wondered if it was wise to give up my 'know for sure how much you will make' hourly situation. After all, the steadiness of my income was what had made the difference to this point. But, I was intrigued by the idea of commission being performance based because my effort would drive my income. I quickly earned the chance to move from Financial Director to General Sales Manager. I was second in command. I loved the challenge. I discovered I was good at training and motivating. Every month I competed with myself to do better than the month before. Having found a place of comfort and plenty I constantly worked harder and harder for "just a little bit more."

Of course, the harder I worked, the more I fought the battle with A-Fib. My oldest son, Michael and my daughter, Mandy eventually started to work for me. It became a joke between us, a sick joke really, that Mom would be to work right after stopping in at the hospital for her fix. Quite often...too often, I would go to the Emergency Room, either late at night or the first thing in the morning and they would begin the intravenous drugs to bring me back into rhythm. In that time frame it was like a light switch. When my heart was out of synch I felt horrible...but when they brought me back to a normal rhythm I was ready to jump into life with a vengeance. Very few people I worked with knew the severity of my health problem. I worked as hard at keeping that a secret as I did at doing a good job in my position.

A Little Deeper

What is 'your' definition of success? Does success encompass more than money, possessions, and financial stability?

God's Word says if we want to eat, we must work. (2 Thessalonians 3:10)

We're also commanded that whatever we do, we are to work at it with our whole heart. (Colossians 3:23)

Read:

> I Timothy 6:6-10
> Proverbs 22:7
> Job 1:21
> Psalm 24:1

Study these Scriptures and their context. Define the balance that you would like in your life relative to success in the space below.

"Dear Lord, I know that I can do nothing without You. I am humbled and brought to my knees with the knowledge that every breathe I take, every beat of my heart is a gift and I know that every good and perfect gift is from You and You alone. Everything that is accomplished in my life is because You love me and sustain me. Thank You for Your goodness, grace, and mercy."

SIX

WHY ME? WHY NOW?

"May my prayer come before you,
turn your ear to my cry.
For my soul is full of trouble and
my life draws near the grave." Psalm 88:2-3

"Hi, Nancy, I hear you're having some Atrial Fibrillation today." I knew most of the cardiologists personally
but this was a new one. I had not met him before. I
began to tell him that things seemed especially severe with
the onset of this episode. I was terribly weak and having
some pain between my shoulder blades. My blood pressure was high. He suspected an aneurysm and sent me
quickly to the hospital for tests. Several hours later the
aneurysm was ruled out and the ER staff began to treat me
like they had countless times before. They got my heart
almost back into rhythm; gave me morphine for my pain
and sent me home.

After vomiting at the hospital, I had another violent
bout of vomiting once I got home. I went to bed, slept
some, and made plans for work the next day. Our General
Manager was gone and this next week would be my chance
to shine. I was really looking forward to steering the ship.

The next morning I got up, took a shower and began to dry my hair. I lost focus in the mirror and realized I was about to pass out. I grabbed the counter and stood with my head down hoping this feeling would pass quickly. I tried to finish my hair but the waves of dizziness kept coming. I sat in my bedroom chair for 15 or 20 minutes and tried to convince myself that I felt some better and tried one more time to stand and get ready for work. This time I did pass out. I was alone in the house...I felt alone in the world.

I was adjusting to my recent divorce. My money-fix-all plan had miserably failed to build the bridge to a stronger marriage...or even an acceptable marriage. Money hadn't stopped the cruelty. It only opened the door for more suspicion and accusation. The paper read, "Irreconcilable Differences." The judicial ring of the words did their best to close the chapter, but failed to spell out the depth of damage and disappointment.

Mandy lived with me but had already left for work. All I could do was cry out, "Lord...Lord." That's all I was able to complete in words...thankfully Scripture tells us that the Holy Spirit is our intercessor, speaking to God, the Father on our behalf. I knew my prayers were finished for me...my plea was communicated.

I decided to call my office and let them know that I would take my one late morning this morning and I would be into work around 11:00 am. I lay back on the bed. I believe I slept for a while. I got myself together about 10:30 and started down the stairs to the garage. On the way down I passed out again. I considered myself to be a pretty tough lady, but this was getting scary. I needed help. I called work and told them I was sick. I tried to minimize the situation to my secretary, but I was crying when I hung up. One of my sales associates heard about my phone call and called me back. Knowing I would probably not, he called for an ambulance and kept me on the phone with him until it arrived.

By the time the EMTs came inside and got me onto a stretcher, my daughter and one of my friends had arrived. They followed the ambulance to the hospital. The ER staff ran me through a couple more tests that morning. Nothing significant showed up in either. Despite my repeated objections, I was admitted. I was in a full-blown A-Fib episode again and just like the day before something seemed severe, different somehow. I couldn't put my finger on it. This time it took more than 8 hours to get me back into normal sinus rhythm. I agreed to stay the night for observation.

The next morning, just before I was to be dismissed, my cardiologist came in and said, "You know, there's one more thing I think we should do before you go home. Let's run an echo-cardiogram." *Good grief, couldn't they get it together and make up their minds...I needed to get to work. It was imperative that I be there. I was just so weak...why? Why was this time so different from what I had grown accustomed to?*

I was familiar with this test. I felt like I could probably do it myself. At least there were no needles involved, no pain to speak of. I listened to the sounds and watched the screen. It was over within a half hour.

As soon as the technician left the room I got up to organize my clothes. I took my cardiologist at his word. He said earlier, "BEFORE you go home." I assumed that after the test I was going to be dismissed. Just as I stepped onto the floor, one of my daughter's friends came in to visit me. Johanna's coming proved to be my second reason for lying back down. My first reason was the dizziness and weakness I hadn't been able to shake. It was a "lie down or fall down decision." I opted to lie. Johanna was talking 90 miles a minute when my doctor walked back in. *Oh, man, this can't be good.* We had already said goodbye earlier that morning. He had given me instructions to see him in his office within the next week. Why was he back? *Dear God...why is he back?*

"Nancy, I've made arrangements to get you downstairs for an angiogram. The echo showed that the left side of your heart is not pumping. We need to take a closer look."

I was numb... all I could do was stare at him. "Did you hear me, Nancy?"

"Yes, okay, how soon?"

"Immediately," was his answer. "I'll see you down there in a few minutes."

"Okay," was all I got out of my mouth. As he turned to walk away I saw the technicians at the door to take me down. Wow! In hospital talk, immediately usually means at least a half hour. Their promptness should have brought comfort to me. I should have been impressed by their dedication and competence. Instead, I was fearful. The fact that they were acting so quickly made me leery. I looked at Johanna and began to cry. It wasn't hysterical crying, just a few tears falling down my cheeks.

She jumped up and out of the way of the technicians. "It's okay", she told me, "I'll call Mandy and Mike...I'll be praying." I was on my way for a test I had hoped– had prayed– never to have. My dad had several angiograms before he died of a heart attack and I was summoning his accounts of the procedure to mind as they wheeled me down the hall. I knew a little bit about what to expect. I also knew if the doctors felt it was necessary to do this test, there might be significant problems. My dad had bypass surgery at the age of 56. I was 49.

I remember the preparation and the kindness of the nursing staff. I remember getting sleepy and subdued. I wasn't comfortable with this. I liked being in charge and in command. This half asleep, half awake state was truly out of my comfort zone and I was afraid. Two cardiologists were present. One was doing the testing and one was standing across from him watching the computer screen. I was watching it too. The difference between us, was that I had no idea what I was seeing. Their conversation was muffled, but I saw what I interpreted as concern and per-haps even confusion on their faces. As I faded in and out I caught part of a conversation. Seemingly my arteries were fine...no blockage, no collapses. Good news...I drifted off with good news. But I awakened with reality. Why was the left side of my heart not pumping? "Nancy, be very still. We have a vice grip cranked down on your leg here to keep pressure on the site." I looked to my right side. Yep, it was a vice grip and the nurse was cranking it tighter.

"What's going on?" I asked.

"The doctor will speak with you when you get back up to your room." Back up to my room? That meant I wasn't going home. I had to go home. I was totally in charge at the dealership...I had to get out of there.

I was in what seemed to be a hallway for some time. My family had arrived and they were allowed to stay with me for a short time. I was quick to tell them I was sure I had heard good news in the heart lab.

"Nancy, we did the angiogram believing that we would find a blockage and we did not."

"Well, that's good news, right?"

"Yes, that's very good news, however..."

Oh, man, that "however" was hanging heavy in the air...what had they found? I watched his mouth from that point, not bringing into focus any other part of his face or expression. It seemed he spoke in slow motion. "What we found instead was evidence that you have had a blood clot pass through your heart. You've suffered a heart attack."

I was confused...in my twenties I had a blood clot pass from my leg to my lung. I recovered relatively quickly from that. He was saying heart attack. My dad suffered several heart attacks and this wasn't the way his happened. He DID have blockages..that's what causes a heart attack..a blockage. What was I hearing?

"There is severe damage to the left side of your heart. We will accelerate the blood thinner a bit and keep a very close eye on you for a few days." He was gone. I was confused.

I turned to my family, "A blood clot and a heart attack aren't the same thing, right? I'm sure it's not as bad as a heart attack. I'm sure everything will be okay." I had reassumed my role as cheerleader, working the crowd, trying to overcome what appeared to be bad news, calming everyone down and reassuring them all was well. I could hear my voice speak the words. Hopefully the words encouraged my loved ones. They did little to penetrate my own fear.

A Little Deeper

Can you recall a time of tragedy....a time when everything in your life fell apart? How did you feel?

Did you feel guilty? Did you feel as if these bad times were a source of punishment from God, justice dealt for some wicked thing you had done?

Somewhere in my background I was programmed to believe a message similar to the one delivered to Job by some of his so-called friends; one that says that all catastrophe comes because of sin. Satan is quick to jump in on those horrific times in our life. He whispers those accusations in our ear when we are at our lowest point. Why do we believe those lies? Where did we get the impression that God is irritated at us and stands at the ever-ready to punish us? On the contrary, God loved us so much he sent His only begotten Son to die for us...to die for our sin. Calvary satisfied that debt. God was satisfied with His Son's work on the cross. We need to shake loose of the idea that despair is a whip in the hand of an angry God.

Instead, when the rain comes, and it surely will come, we need to focus on the true nature of God...on His unconditional love and His matchless grace.

Read:

> 2 Corinthians 4:8
> 2 Corinthians 4:16-18
> Romans 8:28, 33

"Precious Lord, thank you for dying on the cross. Thank you for satisfying my sin debt. Thank you for saving me. Thank you for loving me, watching over me, helping me and guiding me. I need your power in my life. I need your comfort and strength. I'm afraid. I love you, Precious Lord."

SEVEN

FEAR

"The Lord Himself goes before you and will be with you; He
will never leave you nor forsake you.
Do not be afraid; do not be discouraged."
Deuteronomy 31:8

Fear touches all of us in some way. Maybe you
experience fear on some level each and every day. Can you
hear the fear in the following scenarios?

I put together a dynamite resume, but I'm not sure I can actually deliver
   what I promised.
The doctor's office called to set up an appointment, what's wrong?
Bankruptcy is my only way out.
The cost of this medicine keeps going up and up.
My husband just seems so unhappy, so distant, what's going on?
She's four hours late, shouldn't we call the police?
What do you mean not covered? Without the procedure, he'll die.
Do you think he's been hitting her?
I'm so afraid they're going to foreclose on the house.
There's no way we can afford the tuition.
What kind of monster would molest a little child?
I need you to explain what I found in your backpack.
If I'm late again I'll get written up.
I can't do it…I need a drink.

Can you identify with any of these thoughts? If so,

you need no introduction to or definition of FEAR.

Fear is a dangerous and crippling disease. To cripple means *to disable or impair*. We've all been made lame by fear at some point in time. We've all been imprisoned and paralyzed by its grip.

At the close of Deuteronomy, Moses was passing leadership of the Israelites on to Joshua. In the beginning of his own CEO career, he faced crippling, almost debilitating fear. His fear told him that he wasn't capable; he wasn't worthy; he wasn't strong enough for the job God had handed him. Now as he passed on the leadership reigns to Joshua, he recognized the fear gripping this young man who was about to be put in charge of the final trek of the trip into the promise land.

Moses had some parting words, some last minute advice and encouragement for the new man in charge. He repeats himself several times with the phrase, "Be strong and courageous." (vs. 6, 7, and 8) He tells Joshua more than once in chapter 31 "Do not be afraid. Do not be discouraged." Good advice- advice made better when he follows it up by explaining, "You don't have to be afraid because God will never leave you nor forsake you." At the passing of Moses, God Himself reiterates this same advice to Joshua, first in Joshua 1:6 and then again, in verse 7. In verse 9, God's advice becomes a command, "Be strong and courageous. Do not be terrified; do not be discouraged, for the Lord your God will be with you wherever you go." By the end of the chapter, after Joshua has shared the vision, after he has commissioned the people for battle, these same words were used as their "call to fight" in verse 18, "Only be strong and courageous!"

The same words echo in my ear and in my heart. I

know that God is in control. I know that He has promised to be with me wherever I go. He never planned that I should live in fear. His command for my life is no different than it was for Joshua. I hear God say, "Trust me." And I know that when I trust Him...only THEN can I be truly STRONG and COURAGEOUS.

In the hospital, I received a new arrhythmia medication called Sotolol by way of an intravenous tube. A second tube was a fluid drip. After the angiogram I was given instructions not to get up or even raise my head for the next 8 hours. The nursing staff encouraged my kids and my sister to get something to eat and let me sleep for a while. It seems as soon as they left I started coughing. In the beginning it was like a tickle in the back of my throat. It steadily increased in intensity. I asked the nurse for some ice to settle it down, eventually asked for a blanket, asked for the air conditioning to be turned off and finally asked for a cough drop. The more I tried to suppress the cough, the more it persisted. A young nurse came in as the shift changed and I told her something was wrong. I was feeling ill, I couldn't catch my breath, and I couldn't stop coughing. She listened to my lungs and said she would call my doctor. She came back about 15 minutes later and my cardiologist was right behind her. He heard the cough, listened to my lungs and diagnosed that I was having an allergic reaction to the dye used in the angiogram. He ordered a pill; I downed it quickly, hoping for immediate relief.

One of my friends from work came in to see me. I can remember her there and can remember trying to keep a conversation going, but I was really unable to focus. My daughter came back. My mom and step-dad had arrived. I was now gasping for every breath. They must have summoned the nursing staff because soon my little nurse was back, listening to my lungs again.

In a hushed voice she said, "Why can't he hear that?" Without saying anything else, she ran out of the room. By this time I was sweating and shaking. *Please God, help me..please!*

Within minutes my nurse was back with another doctor, a man I had never seen before. He quickly pushed me on my side and began listening to my lungs. I can remember that he asked me to say "tree." When I didn't respond immediately, he barked out again, "Say tree; say it again, again." When he rolled me back the room was full of people and equipment. I wasn't dealing with my fear alone anymore; the entire staff was emanating fear. My family members were rushed out of the room. I watched the eyes of the six people around my bed. I knew instinctively, without any words spoken, that whatever was happening to me was life threatening.

This doctor was taking charge. He issued several orders. I heard, "oxygenating" and heard the word Lasix. A male nurse at the foot of my bed was holding a "resuscitation kit." I knew what it was for and I began to cry. I didn't know who this doctor was or exactly why he was here but I did know that he had heard whatever my nurse had heard earlier. I made eye contact with him and begged him to help me. One of the nurses in the room came toward me with a needle. I watched her inject something into my intravenous tube. My nurse, who had called the "code red," was stroking my forehead. "It's going to be okay. This doctor is a pulmonary specialist. Just breathe slowly, slow, deep breaths." Within 2-3 minutes the Lasix was working...I announced my predicament and the nurse brought in a bed pan. I still wasn't supposed to get up but by this time the world's biggest anxiety attack had me in a neck hold. I couldn't stay on the bed. I asked my daughter to help me to the bathroom. The nurse said, "Oh, no, you can't...well, here, sit here." She shoved a portable potty under me just in time. She checked my groin where they had inserted the needle for the angiogram to make sure it hadn't started to bleed. Within minutes, my cardiologist was back in the room. My back was to him and he bent down and hugged my shoulder. "Nancy, I'm so sorry, this is my fault. You were in heart and lung failure. Your heart wasn't pumping well enough to pump out your fluids. We've stopped the fluids and stopped the Sotalol. They were probably making things worse." It felt so good for someone to hold me, to hug me, and comfort me. I never even thought about how awkward the situation was. He held on to me, I held on to him, and there I was, sitting on the potty...

I never lost consciousness that day. I was aware of everything that had gone on, everything that had been said. It had been a lot of ground to cover, a lot to digest. I learned that in the previous 12 hours I had suffered a heart attack. There was extensive damage to the left side of my heart. Before really coming to grips with that, I had gone into heart and lung failure.

A Little Deeper

In my desparatemenss, I began to pray God's Word. In my state of fear, my extreme anxiety, nothing else would come.

I needed to commune with my Lord, my Abba Father, and my own words failed me. So I prayed His words.

"Even though I walk through the valley of the shadow of death, I will fear no evil, for You are with me." (Psalm 23:4)

"You will keep in perfect peace him whose mind is steadfast, because he trusts in you." (Isaiah 26:3)

Have you prayed through any specific verses from the Bible, applying them to yourself?

What prompted your "praying through God's Word?" Which verses did you pray?

Turn to the book of Psalms and find a passage that closely parallels with how you're feeling right now. Use God's Words to communicate your praise, your heartache, and your petition.

Consider these verses:

Psalm 17: 8   Psalm 18:3
Psalm 51:1-3   Psalm 18: 3
Psalm 54:17   Psalm 55:1-5

"Oh, God, You are my refuge and strength, my ever-present help in trouble (Ps 46:1). Hear my cry for mercy as I call to You for help. (Ps 28:2) You are my strength and my shield; my heart trusts in You and I am helped. (Ps 28:7)"

EIGHT

CALL THE FAMILY

"The waves of death swirled about me; the torrents of destruction overwhelmed me. The cords of the grave coiled around me; the snares of death confronted me. In my distress I called to the Lord; I called out to my God. From His temple he heard my voice; my cry came to his ears."
2 Samuel 22:3-7

Oh no...no, no, Lord, NO! I raised my head slightly. I raised my hand to my chest. I fought for breath. My entire upper body was shaking and vibrating. It was back...back with a vengeance. *I'm too weak, Lord...I can't handle this now...no, please, no, I can't be in A-Fib again. It's too much, too soon....Lord, I'm afraid. This time it will surely kill me."*

It had only been three or four hours since the peak of my last terrorizing event. Ten to twelve pounds of water had been drained from my system, clearing my heart and lungs of the fluid that threatened to drown me. I was able to breathe again. The heaviness in my chest and the sense of suffocation were gone now. I was allowing myself to believe that this particular situation was at least somewhat under control. All my family and friends had said goodnight, kissed me, prayed with me, and gone home, all except for Mandy. She insisted that she stay the night. The nursing staff brought in a reclining type chair to make her more comfortable.

The lights flipped on; nurses flooded the room. "Nancy, Nancy, lie back. No, no, you can't get up." Almost as bad as the A-Fib itself is the anxiety that grips your mind and body with the onset of the arrhythmia. The "fight or flight" syndrome kicks in. It's so hard to be still. And, of course, being still and quiet was what everyone wanted me to be at that moment. "We're calling your doctor right now." Mandy was up and out of her chair and at my bedside arranging the sheets and blanket back up over my body. She gently pushed my shoulder, encouraging me back onto the bed. I watched her as she went through the motions of calming me, making me comfortable. I can remember studying her features, drinking in every detail of her face. I needed to be aware; I needed to hold onto this moment in time. I asked her to sing to me.

Through the years singing with my kids had been one of the things that brought me joy, peace and comfort. Mandy has a beautiful voice. I needed to hear her sing. I know it must have seemed like a crazy request. The confusion and fear showed up on her face. She tried...I can remember she tried so hard, but the tears overtook both of us. The nurses asked her to move to the other side of the bed. They were once again injecting medication into my intravenous tube. "What's that?" I had learned the importance of being vitally involved in my own care. I can remember one of the nurses answered, and I thought she said "Cortisone." Why in the world would they be giving me cortisone? Wasn't that for pain? "Wait, why?" I asked.

"We're going to try to get you back into sinus rhythm," was her reply. I know I asked again what they were giving me, but I don't remember their response. I found out later she had said, "Cordarone."

This episode was different, worse than any I had had before. Every breath felt as if it might be my last. Fear paralyzed me. I didn't believe I would make it through the night. I thought about my family. I needed my loved ones to be there. After having been divorced for a little over a year...after a bitter, ugly turmoil involving restraining orders, unkind, hateful and hurtful words and actions, I needed to see my husband of 28 years. I thought it would be best if he were here with the kids. I asked Mandy to call everyone. She didn't hesitate. She had been my best friend throughout my illness, throughout the painful last years of my marriage, throughout my struggle to climb the corporate ladder. She probably knew me better than anyone else. She knew instinctively that I believed I was dying.

That night was without a doubt the longest of my life. My blood pressure dropped to dangerously low levels. It wasn't enough that I could feel it dropping, I was hooked to a monitor equipped with an obnoxious beep that gave warning at each new dip. The alarm made us acutely aware of the severity of the problem. Several other machines monitored my situation and the nursing staff was ever present. I hung on to every minute, not wanting to close my eyes for even a second. This wasn't the first time I had faced death. This wasn't the first time I experienced this "struggle to stay alive" state of mind. I think there's a spirit within all of us that fights for the last breath. I knew my life was in God's hands and I also knew death would usher me into His great Heaven, still the desperation raged.

My doctor came in around 5:00 a.m. He told me he wasn't surprised that I had gone back into A-Fib. He explained that the problem was two-fold. The left side of my heart wasn't pumping and the large amount of Lasix used to clear the fluid from around my heart drained the electrolytes from my system. Either scenario would have been enough to cause arrhythmia, but the presence of both made it inevitable.

I was glad to see him. I was glad to be seeing anyone. I told him I was afraid I was dying and begged him to help me. He left me with assurance that they were doing all they could. The priority at this point was to try to get my heart back into sinus rhythm. He didn't want to have to cardio-convert me. Electro cardio-conversion is a last-ditch method of righting arrhythmias. It was a drastic measure and he wasn't sure I was strong enough to withstand the stress. He made it clear, however, there would be no other choice if things failed to improve within the next 24 hours. The situation was grim. In the previous 24 hours I had faced death twice and now in this exaggerated state of A-Fib and low blood pressure, I didn't have the strength to fight the battle one more time. The onslaughts were coming too close together. *Oh, dear God, get me through this. Please God, don't let me die...please help me.*

My family began to pour in. My ex-husband was there. I could tell that he too thought I wouldn't make it through the day. I read his face and the face of everyone else that walked through the door. Such fear; such sorrow and pain washed over all of us. How does one prepare for death? How do I say goodbye? How do I tell them that I have loved them, with all my heart, with all my being? How do I let go?

I actually don't recall being moved but my next memories take place in a private room in the intensive care cardiac wing. Both Michael and Mandy lived close by and they were there. Matthew was on his way from Pennsylvania where he was working as an associate pastor. My family had gathered chairs and made a half circle vigil around my bed. Other visitors poured in and out of the room throughout the morning. I knew this wasn't the norm for intensive care. I knew that visitors were usually limited. I surmised that the bend in the rules was because the staff was allowing me my chance to say goodbye. I can remember responding to my family, talking to each one of them but still praying, silently praying, *Lord, please don't let me die. I'm afraid...so afraid. I need a miracle..I'm trusting you for a miracle. I belong to you. I know that you have a plan for me...a plan for my best.* (Jer. 29:11).

My family kept watching the machines that watched me. I didn't need to SEE them. I could feel the chaos going on inside me. I felt as if the entire bed was quaking. My heart was racing. Without seeing the numbers registered on the machines, I knew from experience they were recording a rate somewhere between 250 and 300 beats per minute. I could tell that my family members, not on the same familiar terms with this disease as I was, were shocked as they watched the monitor. Even though I was on oxygen, every breath was a struggle. In retrospect, I probably should have been using what we all believed to be my last breaths to say the proper goodbyes, to make my final wishes known, share my "last will and testament" with those gathered around me. Instead, I found myself trying to calm the spirit in the room, trying to reassure everyone. I was smiling, trying to look alert and in control. I couldn't bear to see the people I loved hurting. I had to make it better. *Lord, help me make it better for them...they're so upset.*

I lasted through the day. Matt had arrived. *Thank you, Lord.* I so needed to see him. Somehow it brought peace to everyone that he was there. I can remember thinking it was so unfair that he was immediately thrown into a pastoral role, as if he was expected to have all the right Scriptures for us to ponder, the answers and prayers that would miraculously make everything better and bring peace to everyone in the middle of this trial. He was, in fact, simply a son grieving for what seemed to be an inevitable situation that he wasn't prepared to face.

The senior partner of the cardiology group came into the room. *Oh, the big guns are here, Lord. Is this it?* He walked over to edge of my bed, looked at me and then up to the monitors. "Nancy, you've had a rough couple of days."

"Yeah, I sure have," I agreed.

"Well, here's our plan. We've already started you on a new medication called Cordarone. We're going to continue a heavy down-load of this drug." He further explained that this was an end-of-the road effort. He believed it was an extreme measure that came with a long list of risks and side effects, but we were in an end-of-the road situation. He spent some time counseling me, educating me, and seeing no other alternative. I agreed to the suggested plan. He spoke to my family, turned toward the door to walk away, and then turned back. "We need to clear this room. Nancy needs to rest. I understand she hasn't slept for more than 48 hours. I'm going to give her something for sleep." Everyone was quick to jump into compliance. He returned in less than a minute with a "NO VISITORS" sign and posted it on the door. *Oh, Lord, this is Hope. I'm hearing Hope..thank you..thank you!*

Tentative smiles had replaced the worried creases on the faces of my loved ones. They had heard it too. It was HOPE. They needed to leave and get some rest themselves. Now they could do that and they could leave with HOPE. *Thank you, Lord..Thank you!* The doctor was serious about me getting some sleep. I swallowed the tiny pills, allowed the nurses to lower the head of my bed, and I closed my eyes. They stayed closed for several hours.

A Little Deeper

Psalm 63:7 declares that God is our Help.

"Because You are my help, I sing in the shadow of Your wings." Psalm 63:7

Uncover other descriptions of God within the verses that follow:

Psalm 144:2 declares that God is _____ _____,

_____, _____, _____,

_____

Psalm 61:3 declares that God is our _____ and

_____ _____.

Psalm 19:14 declares that God is our _____

and our _____.

Psalm 27:1 declares that Lord is our _____

and _____ and the _____

of my life.

"Dear Lord, You are truly all I need. You are everything to me. Forgive me when I run to any other hiding places. Forgive me when my faith wavers. Your Word says you are for me...You are on my side, so, who can be against me. I thank You for Your power, for Your mercy, for Your grace. I trust You, Lord. Help me trust You more."

NINE

TRUST

But I trust in you, O Lord; I say,
"You are my God." Psalm 31:14

Day three arrived. I awoke trying to assess my condition. My heart rate was still irregular but it had slowed down. This was good. I was breathing better. This was good. Someone walked in with a breakfast tray. This was good. You feed patients who are going to recover. This was very good. The doctors made their rounds early. They were encouraged by my improvement and continued the down-load of medication. I was allowed occasional visitors two at a time and by the end of the day I was getting up out of bed to walk to the bathroom. On the fourth day I took a stand up shower and walked down the hall to talk with friends and family who were gathered in the waiting room.

My heart rate was still elevated, now ranging between 80 and 150 beats per minute and I was still in arrhythmia. I knew time was running out. If I didn't convert to normal rhythm on my own, they would be forced to get out the paddles. That evening one of the doctors told me that since I was improving they would give the new medication until noon the next day to do its work. If by then I had not converted they would take me down for electro cardio-conversion.

I prayed even more fervently that night. I had regained some strength and used it to plead with the Lord. *Please help me convert..please help me. I'm so afraid of the electro conversion...please control this thing so I don't have to go through that. You are the Great Physician..I trust you to hear me and answer my prayer.*

The staff came in on the 5th day with a breakfast tray. I was delighted to have, at least sort of, slept through the night. I fully expected to wake in good rhythm. I was frustrated to find that I had not. Just as I took the lid off the breakfast plate a nurse came rushing in and reclaimed the tray. I didn't have to ask why. I knew that if I was going down to be cardio-converted that I shouldn't have anything to eat. It was 8:30 and they were obviously making plans for the procedure.

Much like Elijah (I Kings 19), hiding from the queen, I began to pout. So far, I hadn't had time for the pity party but now I was opening that door. I had seen God step in and spare my life, not once, but twice, in the past 5 days and now it seemed as if He had forgotten me. *Doesn't He see me? Doesn't He know I've had all I can bear?*

In I Kings we find Israel in a mess. They have taken their eyes off the true and living God. They are in spiritual and moral decay. In walks a man named Elijah. He's a common man, with common abilities, from the common town of Tishbe. In chapter 17 Elijah orchestrated his own "mission impossible." He completed an assignment for God Almighty. Armed with the sacred truth that little is much when God is in it, he delivers a message to King

Ahab. In I Kings 17:1, Elijah boldly stands before the king and says, "As the Lord, the God of Israel lives, whom I serve, there will be neither dew nor rain in the next few years except at my word." He's not just playing weatherman here, he's predicting drought, famine, starvation and death. He hits the scene with uncommon boldness and bravery. No, he wasn't common after all. What a superhero! He not only heard and understood the message of God; he fearlessly unfolded that message to a less than receptive King. It's never easy to communicate an unpopular opinion to a hostile crowd, but Elijah was putting his very life at stake here.

Wow, what must it be like to be an Elijah...to possess that kind of faith and strength...to be able to exercise that kind of obedience? Look at his performance on Mount Carmel in chapter 18. Representing God Almighty's team, he brings home the "gold." He takes on the 450 prophets of Baal, and the 400 prophets of Asherah to boot. He taunts the opposing team in verse 27 as they are beseeching their Gods to send fire from heaven to burn their sacrifice. Then he stacks the cards against himself even further by watering down his own alter in verses 33-35. In the end he calls on the Name of the Lord, asking Him to prove himself to these people one more time. As a result, fire falls from heaven and burns up the sacrifice, the wood, the stones, and the soil. Just to polish things off we are told in verse 38 that the flames licked up even the water in the trench.

About the time we decide men and women in the Old Testament have an edge on this faith thing, we read on. What's going on in Elijah's life in chapter 19? King Ahab runs home to cry on his wife's shoulder about all that has taken place on Mount Carmel. Her name is Jezebel and she's not a nice lady. We have account in chapter 18 that she has hunted down and killed scores of God's prophets. Now as Elijah steps away from great victory on that mountain top, he gets a message that Jezebel has sworn to kill him as well. That's laughable, right? This is Elijah... super-hero of the hour. But wait...verse 3 of chapter 19 says, "Elijah was afraid and ran for his life." How can that be? What changed? Was he common after all... common like you and me? When we take our eyes off God and give in to fear, all we can see is despair and defeat. And like Elijah, we throw ourselves a pity party.

My brother, his wife and son came in to see me around 11:00. They were on their way to a ball game. I wanted to ask them to stay with me. I wanted to shout out that I was afraid. I wanted to cry. I wanted to lean on them...have them hold me, comfort me. But instead I spoke confidently, assuring them that all was well.

After they left I had some time to talk to God.

Lord, I'm still in awe knowing that you chose to spare me. I know beyond a shadow of a doubt that You intervened. I know that you didn't save my life just to let me die during a common procedure like a cardio conversion. They do it every day, right? Scores of lives have been saved with those paddles. Why am I so afraid of this...I'm just being a big baby. I'm sorry. Forgive me. I know you must hate it when I whine. I should be praising you, not complaining. I trust you. It'll be okay...just hold me in your arms. I trust you...I trust you...I trust you.

At 11:45 am, like a light switch, my heart jumped back into sinus rhythm. I knew it before the nurses saw it on the monitor.   I smiled as two of them walked in. "You know, right?" one of them asked.

"Oh yeah, I know," I answered. "Well, we had things set up for you to go downstairs...looks like we won't have to do that this morning. We'll let your doctor know." They were gone. I was alone...no one to turn to, no one to rejoice with, and no one to cry with.   Trying to stay calm and still, I bowed my head and thanked God.

A Little Deeper

Can you remember a time when you could only see despair?

Can you remember a time when you felt as if God wasn't listening?

Consider the following verses:

> The LORD is far from the wicked but he hears the prayer of the righteous. Proverbs 15:29

> This is the confidence we have
> in approaching God:
> that if we ask anything according to his will,
> he hears us. 1 John 5:14

> He fulfills the desires of those who fear him; he hears their cry and saves them. Psalm 145:19

The righteous cry out, and the LORD hears them; he delivers them from all their troubles.
Psalm 34:17

"Oh, Lord, who am I that I should gain audience with the King of King and Lord of Lords? To know that You see me...to know that You hear me is beyond my comprehension, but I know that it's true. I know that you care about the tiniest details of my life and you will never leave me or forsake me. I praise You for Your goodness to me!"

TEN

ANXIETY AT THE HELM

"I lift up my eyes to the hills –where does my help come from?
My help comes from the Lord, the Maker of heaven and earth."
Psalm 121:1,2

My cardiologist made rounds early on the sixth day. He opened the conversation with, "Well, Nance, things are looking better than when I saw you last. I hope you're not in a hurry to run back to work?" He knew me too well. I told him I would like to get back quickly but realized that I didn't have the strength to go for at least a couple of days. "Nancy, you've had a heart attack. On top of that, you went into heart and lung failure. This last couple of days you've been receiving mega doses of this new medication and you're just now back into a good solid sinus rhythm. You've got to give yourself time here."

"Oh, sure," I said. "How much time do you think?" "I don't want to dangle a time frame in front of you... recovery time is different for everyone. Obviously you're strong, let's just give it some time and see." Not satisfied with that answer I pressured him.

"Yeah, I am strong, so I should be able to go back in at least a week or so, right?"

He didn't give in to my attempts at pressure, "You have someone to care for you at home, right?"

"Yes, my daughter lives with me."

"Good. I'm going to sign you up for recovery therapy. It's here at the hospital." He gave me a brochure and told me I could pick from various time and date slots. "I strongly encourage you to work with these people. It'll help you regain strength. Let's see how that goes and we'll talk about a release date when I see you in my office in two weeks."

Good grief...it seemed like my doctor was trying out for some new Olympic category; competing for the "shortest time spent with a patient" medal. He was in like a flash and out like a half a flash. I had questions. Was I to understand that I was going to have to wait two weeks to be able to ask them? I was having a hard time digesting all that had taken place and couldn't make sense of what was ahead.

When Mandy came in that morning she was flipping through the same brochure the doctor had left me earlier. I told her they were dismissing me and she began gathering up my things. The nurses were in and out with papers to be signed and before I knew it I was being wheeled to the front door where Mandy waited under the hospital awning. I was going home. This was good. *"Thank you, Lord."*

It felt good to be in my own home. When I had left a little over week before, I wasn't sure if I would ever come home again. But now, praise God, here I was. I was sure to recover quicker here in my house, in my room, in my bed. Surely everything would be okay... surely...surely...

That night I couldn't sleep. I couldn't close my eyes.

I wouldn't lie down because I felt as though I couldn't breathe. Mandy moved into my bedroom and slept beside me because I was so afraid. Again, like Elijah, coming out of great victory, I was now vulnerable, uneasy, worried. Having faced my own mortality, I was gripped with fear and paranoia. This wasn't like me. I was by nature an optimist, a "look for the silver-lining" kind of gal. Now I couldn't move without extreme fear. I couldn't sleep. I couldn't rest. I was afraid...so afraid.

That night, and several nights after, I walked the floor, pacing from the living room to the kitchen to the dining room and back again, and back again, and back again. Wave after wave of dizziness kept washing over me. I drifted in and out of coherence. I felt every heart beat. I seemingly struggled with every breath. I called the doctor's office almost every day. We adjusted and re-adjusted medications. My blood pressure was up and down.

In the beginning, my job- my career- had been first and foremost in my mind. Now arrangements had been made for a leave of absence and my first and foremost thought was to "just stay alive." I'd never known such fear. I prayed like never before. I memorized verses and recited them over and over, trying to regain some bit of composure and control. I prayed God's Word. Mandy read to me at night. We picked out a devotional book and she would read it to me, much like a mother reads to a child, hoping to infuse calm and quiet, hoping that I would be able to settle down and sleep.

I didn't know it then, but later learned, I was having extreme anxiety attacks. My recovery was slow and when I didn't see the progress I expected, I fell into deep depression and experienced anxiety that would cause chest pain, elevated pulse rate, sweating, dizziness, and nausea.

Depression and anxiety were new to me. Not recognizing them for what they were, I contributed all the feelings I was experiencing to my heart problems. I was sure I was in congestive heart failure. I had tightness in my chest on a daily basis. I couldn't seem to combat the fatigue and weakness that plagued me. I was confined to bed rest, but no matter how hard I tried, I couldn't stay there. I thought if I stayed in bed, I would surely die.

I made at least two trips back to the emergency room during the first two weeks after having been dismissed. One night I experienced such a vicious attack of dizziness and shortness of breath that I asked Mandy to call an ambulance. My heart rate was elevated and irregular. The EMTs were concerned so they rushed me to the hospital, sirens screaming and lights flashing. After I was examined, hooked up to machines, tracked and monitored, the doctor told me he could admit me for observation or he could give me something to settle me down and I could go home and rest there. I knew if I stayed they would make me stay in bed and I didn't know if I could do that. I opted to go home. He prescribed a medication called Ativan. My daughter and I got the prescription filled before we left the hospital. This was the beginning of a 6-year addiction to prescription medication, but at that moment in time I needed the help and it proved to bring wonderful relief for the anxiety that had been ruling my existence during the eternally long days and nights since my heart attack.

One tiny pill, smaller than my pinkie nail, and I could sleep...actually settle down and sleep. It was wonderful for me and it had to be just as wonderful for Mandy.

What a trooper she had been. Healing comes with rest and I had until that point been unable to allow my body the rest it craved. This tiny little pill helped me grab hold of the "old me." I was once again able to approach life with reason and logic. I could focus. I could think things through. But most of all, I could rest.

I began a daily journal. I wrote in detail how I felt each day. I wrote down my prayers and the answers to my prayers I had seen and was continuing to see as the days passed. I praised God over and over again for the way He had orchestrated my care and for the fact that I was still alive. I wrote down all the things I wanted to do before I died. I set up goals, outlined "how to" plans for making dreams happen, compiled mission statements. I made it a priority to attend church again. The heart attack came in early October, shortly after my 49th birthday. By the end of November I was hand crafting Christmas presents for friends and loved ones. This was progress. This was good.

I was, of course, concerned about how I would function with part of my heart not working. I didn't know what to expect from day to day. Having been told about the critical damage, I couldn't quite get my mind around it. I knew I would never be the same, but hoped that I would be able to live at least a somewhat normal life. The recovery therapy was good for me. I added my own exercise program and was determined to regain optimum strength...whatever that was. I continually asked my doctor what my expectations should be. He scheduled an echocardiogram in mid December to further study the damage to my heart so that he could address all my questions.

A Little Deeper

Can you recall a time in your life when things looked absolutely bleak, irreparable, and irreversible? Call your despair by its name. Was it spiritual, physical, emotional, financial, relational?

2 Corinthians 4:8 says,

> "We are hard pressed on every side, but not crushed; perplexed, but not in despair, persecuted, but not abandoned; struck down, but not destroyed."

Verse 16-18 continues,

> "Therefore we do not lose heart. Though outwardly we are wasting away, yet inwardly we are being renewed day by day. For our light and momentary troubles are achieving for us an eternal glory that far outweighs them all. So we fix our eyes not on what is seen, but on what is unseen. For what is seen is temporary, but what is unseen is eternal."

There have been volumes written about how crucial it is to "keep our eyes" fixed on Jesus. Peter is the one we think of first when we look for that perfect example of keeping our focus on the Master.

Matthew 14:25-32 tells the story of Jesus walking on the water. Peter said to the Lord, "If it's you, tell me to come to you on the water." Jesus said, "Come." So in verse 29, Peter steps out of the boat. There was no lack of faith at that point. Peter believed Jesus could sustain him. Had he not believed, he wouldn't have been able to get out of the boat. But then adversity comes. The wind picks up and steals Peter's focus. Verse 30 tells us that all of a sudden, he was afraid and began to sink.

When the wind of adversity blows in our lives, we react much like Peter. The trouble we experience is all we see. Jesus whispers to our heart,

"You of little faith, why did you doubt?"
Matthew 14:31

"Oh, Lord, help me learn to keep my eyes on you. When the storms are brewing all around me increase my faith. Purge my unbelief; forgive my fear. Let me walk on the water with You, Lord. Draw me close, I pray."

ELEVEN

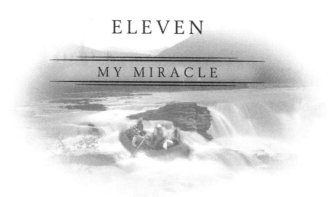

MY MIRACLE

"Be strong and take heart, all you who
hope in the Lord." Psalm 31:24

I was nervous. I had prayed for full recovery, but
logic told me that it wasn't likely. It seemed too much to
ask. I prayed that I could somehow go on, forget the
damage, at least not think about it every day. I prayed to
have some semblance of normality. I prayed about my
future. I prayed about my quality of life. I was alone now
and needed to support myself. I needed to help Mandy
finish college. I needed to be able to find the strength and
stamina to go on.

I was exercising every day. My home office was filled
with five different contraptions, everything from a tread-
mill to a bow-flex. The day of my echo appointment I rode
my bicycle to the doctor's office, probably about 5 or 6
miles. I'm not sure why it was so important for me to do
that. I remember wanting to brag to my cardiologist that
I had done it and I needed him to praise me for my efforts
in regaining my strength. I felt like I would get extra
points for trying harder and maybe there would be some
miraculous reward waiting for me down the road.

I was taken to the heart lab where a technician was waiting, and we got started immediately. I watched the screen; I listened to the sounds; I worried. When we were finished, I waited in one of the conference rooms for my cardiologist. When he walked in, he was smiling. It took me by surprise. He just wasn't a "smilie" kind of guy. "Nancy, I watched this twice, once by myself and once with the technician." That was his opening remark. *Okay, where are we going...he's still smiling.* "As remarkable as it sounds, after all you've been through, there's no evidence of damage to your heart at this time. You have total function!" I wasn't following. "That's good, right?" I interrupted. "It's better than good," he said, "it's miraculous!" I was tentative...he had to convince me. He told me he watched the cassette twice and had also compared it to my last echo done in the hospital and reviewed the angiogram done at that time as well.

No damage at all...where there had been damage before...how could that be? What are the odds of that happening? I was reminded of the story in Acts chapter 12 about a group that had gathered to pray for Peter who was in prison. These faithful prayer warriors were sincerely, earnestly praying for his release. They were praying for nothing less than a miracle. A young girl in the house answered a knock at the door and announced to the group that it was Peter. They said she must be mistaken because, after all, Peter was in jail. He couldn't possibly be at the front door. Even though the reason for their coming together was to pray for Peter and his release, they were skeptical about the answer to their prayers.

I too was having momentary disbelief...what was wrong with me? Why was I looking for an explanation I could touch and handle? Why was I second guessing this news, this wonderful, miraculous news? Why did I find it necessary to limit God, reduce Him to what I could handle in my own mind?

I had an opportunity to swim in a "hallelujah pool" but I was wasting time wading around in doubt and confusion. Why is it that we pray for miracles and we are quick to testify that we believe in miracles, yet when one comes our way we dissect it, we weigh it? We stack it up beside our measurement stick of logic. We tear it apart piece by piece, looking for reasonable and justifiable answers for the outcome before we jump in and just do what we were created to do...Give God the Glory!

Probably seeing my unbelief, my tentative non-response, the doctor reiterated again, "Nancy you are whole, you are well! I usually am the bearer of bad news but this time I get to be the one to say...you are well! It's time to jump back into life. With this new medication preventing your A-Fib and with no permanent damage to your heart, this can be the first day of the rest of your life." My mind was spinning...*yes, the first day of the rest of my life...yes...YES!*

The weather had taken a turn. When I left the doctor's office on my bike, it was windy and the temperature had dropped at least 20 degrees. I cried all the way home. The tears were beginning to freeze on my cheeks when I finally pedaled into my driveway.

Who do I call first? I needed to rejoice with my loved ones. I needed to share my news and shout my praise. This was real miracle stuff. I wondered if anyone would believe me. Putting it into words sounded suspicious somehow. I decided it wasn't up to me to make people believe. My job, my JOY, was just to give praise.

I had already told my boss that I wouldn't be able to return to work. I had made arrangements to pick up my final check. Was it too late...could I turn that situation around? I had to try. I made the call. I told him I had made a mistake and I wanted my job back. He had already filled my position and seemingly it would have been better to just leave things as they were. Yet, he graciously welcomed me back and I re-entered the work force the first of January.

Two weeks of a part time schedule flew by. Mid-January brought me back, face to face with long hours and high expectations. I was doing better every day. I was regaining strength. Because my new medication was keeping me in sinus rhythm I perhaps was even stronger than before. *Thank you Lord!*

A Little Deeper

Do you watch the HGTV channel? I love those makeover shows where they transform broken down, ugly, outdated, seemingly hopeless houses into virtual show cases. I so admire the people who can walk into these dilapidated, unworthy, un-wanted structures and see hope. They have the vision to see what could be. They have the patience to take on the labor of love. They don't stop with just saving the house; they transform it into something beautiful, something special. They knock out walls; replace floors, plumbing, cabinets. They paint. They tweak and hover until it's magnificent...until it's a place anyone would be proud to call home.

I praise God that he saw me in my need, and He bought me...He paid the price for my salvation. I praise Him that I belong to Him and as His child He continues to tweak and hover over me because I matter to him. He has plans for me...plans to prosper me, not to harm me. (Jeremiah 29:11)

Can you recall the time when God reached down in mercy and saved your soul? Have you accepted Him as your personal Savior? Where were you? How old were you? Talk about your own personal transformation. Talk about how the Lord in grace continues to bring about that extreme makeover in your life.

If you have never accepted the Lord Jesus Christ as your Savior, don't wait another day. Luke 19:10 says, "For the Son of Man came to seek and to save what was lost." The Lord is looking for you. He longs to hear you call His name. Being born again only requires that you ask. Ask Him today...right now. Acts 16:31 says, "Believe in the Lord Jesus, and you will be saved." You can pray a prayer as simple as this, "Dear Lord, I believe You are Christ, the Son of the living God. I ask you to forgive my sin and come into my heart and into my life. Be my Savior and my Lord. Amen." Be sure to talk to another Christian about your decision. God Bless you as you walk with Him! I love the old southern gospel song that says, "He saw not what I was, He saw what I could be."

"I give thanks to You, mighty Lord, for You are good...Your have done a work of great wonder...Your love endures forever! (Psalm 136) I walked in the midst of trouble but You preserved my life. I trust You to fulfill Your purpose for me...Your love endures forever! (Psalm 138:7-8). I praise you Lord!"

TWELVE

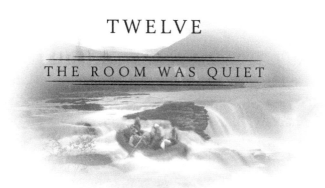

THE ROOM WAS QUIET

"The Lord your God has blessed you in all the work
of your hands. He has watched over your journey ....
The Lord your God has been with you, and you
have not lacked anything." Deuteronomy 2: 7

The room was quiet...so quiet. But what a beautiful, exquisite room it was. How was it I found myself here, living in this beautiful home? For most of my life I drove through neighborhoods like this and hated the people behind the brick walls. Somewhere along the way I stopped hating and decided I could live in one of these neighborhoods. I only needed to apply myself. I bought into the American dream. I was a living, breathing poster girl for the "Be All You Can Be" slogan. I lived out the "Conceive it-Believe it-Achieve it" concept; I dug in my heels and persevered. I deserved this. I had "arrived."

What an honor to have been asked to step up and open a new branch of the auto division in the neighboring state. I had worked myself up from Office Manager to Finance Manager, to General Sales Manager and now I had the opportunity of moving north to the neighboring state to work as the General Manager of a brand new facility.

This was beyond exciting. This was the break I had been waiting for.

My first reward (from me to me) was this house. It was too big. The payments were too high. I knew I wouldn't stay in it long enough to pay it off. At best, it was temporary. But that didn't stop me. It was my dream home. It was spectacular. I wanted to live here...just to know what it would be like to live here. I reasoned that it was a good investment. I was here by myself most of the time. Mandy had moved up to Wyoming with me, but she had her friends and activities. I didn't see too much of her. Michael lived back in Colorado. Matt was in Pennsylvania. And the room was very quiet.

It's okay, I told myself...soon I would relish these quiet moments. We were opening a sales facility in the mall. We would get the business underway there while we waited for the new building to be completed. I knew this endeavor would require everything I could muster but I lived for these kinds of challenges. I was good at this and finally I had a chance to prove myself...show them what I could do, what I could accomplish.

We were selling cars at 10:00 A.M. the first day we opened the doors in the mall. There were two of us, myself and a young man who had caught the vision and made the decision to move his family of five to become a part of this enterprise. Within only a couple of months, I brought another man on board and began interviewing for positions that were opening up quicker than I could fill them. It was an exciting time in my life. I lived and breathed the business. I was not only deep into building a strong team, I was ultimately responsible for profitability. The mall was open from 10:00 A.M. to 9:00 P.M. so we had to match those hours. I usually showed up between 8:00 and 8:30 A.M. Most nights I stayed until after 9:00 P.M. We were right across from the theatres and I wanted to be there to help handle the crowd that wandered over after the movies. There was no room for life outside this business. I had one focus and one focus only. This was my chance to shine, my opportunity to make my mark.

The new arrhythmia medication was my "miracle of the moment." I was also taking the blood thinner, Coumadin. At this point in time this particular recipe seemed to be managing my disease well. It had been a year since my heart attack and a year with no extreme A-Fib episodes. Unbelievable!

Although I couldn't keep up with where my mind was spinning with the jobs and projects I set out for myself, I was pleased with my energy and endurance level. There were only a handful of women across the nation in a General Manager position in an automobile dealership. Most of them had family ties to management. I didn't. I had to earn the right to be in charge. I had to prove myself anew and afresh every day. I couldn't just meet expectations. I had to exceed. The business totally consumed me. I had no social life. I wasn't active in church. I had no close friends. My drive to succeed was pushing everything and everyone else to the sidelines. I had less and less time for my children, my friends, my family and, yes, even less time for God. My priorities were skewed out of proportion. I lived in a vacuum, struggling to perform at a higher and higher level, achieving more, acquiring more.

Some would say it's the fear of being outdone, outsmarted, fear of loosing position and status that drives us.

I'm not sure why I was running so hard or where this insatiable driving force originated from. I don't remember being fearful of failure. I was confident about my abilities and anxious to perform. Seemingly I had something to prove. I hadn't received much affirmation in my life and I took great pleasure in the praise and the sense of achievement that was pinned to each successful week or month or year in business. I think that approval was almost as important as the money I earned.

There's nothing inherently wrong with climbing the corporate ladders of success, reaching goals, or acquiring material possessions. However, in retrospect I can see that in my case, my personal sense of significance was tied too closely to achieving. I found my identity in what I did for a living. I understand now that God's plan for me entails a far more stable basis for significance. My identity, my value, and security only find meaning because of my relationship with Him.

The next few years I continued my ascent up the ladder, the ladder I believed would lead to more money, more authority, and more success. It was in these years I began to hear God whispering to my heart to 'move on'. I know now He was gently calling me, preparing me, directing me to a place of service for His glory. I felt the pull but was confused by it and fearful of it. So I dismissed it, packed it away in the dark trunk of my mind and kept driving the route I had highlighted on my own road map.

The book of Deuteronomy gives account of the Israelites in the land of Moab. They were on the other side of the Jordan River, just about to cross. They had actually been this close before. In the book of Numbers, forty years earlier, they had this same vantage point, but because of fear and unbelief, they failed to move forward and claim the Promised Land. They chose instead to be stagnant, stick with what they knew. They were so fearful they asked in Numbers 13:3, "Wouldn't it be better for us to go back to Egypt?" They were willing to settle for the worthlessness, the bondage and oppression because it was familiar to them. Four decades later Moses reminded the Israelites of the choice they had made. In the first chapter of Deuteronomy, verse 31, he says, "...you saw how the Lord your God carried you, as a father carries his son." Despite God's provision and His promises, they had refused to trust Him for the rest of the journey. Because of their unbelief, they wandered around in circles for the next forty years.

We have the promise that, "The Lord God goes before us and fights for us." (Deut 1:30) We've witnessed His presence in our lives when He's carried us through the battles and the storms. We know that the victories come because of His power and provision. Even so, like the children of Israel, we often find ourselves at the next crossroad, shaking out our own map, operating out of our own reserves. Influenced by fear and disbelief, we hesitate to follow God in a new direction.

One kind of fear drove me, another kind of fear kept me captive in my own, self-imposed prison. Because of the conflicting fears dueling in my mind, I chose, like the children of Israel, to keep wandering. I continued to look for lasting fulfillment within my job and my position. This was a season in my life when I didn't have to spend every waking moment worrying about my health. It was liberating in so many ways. I felt as if the weight of the world had been lifted. So because I was able, I pushed the envelope, stretching myself to unreasonable limits.

A Little Deeper

Are you driven? Do you throw caution to the wind and run in overdrive, ever in the pursuit of 'more'? What do you sacrifice in order to keep up the pace?

Read Matthew 6:33.

In the Book of Ecclesiastes, Solomon poses similar questions. This short, 12-chapter book has sometimes been called a cynical, uninspiring, pessimistic book. But as we take a close look, what we find is a man going through great emotional turmoil, a highly intelligent, articulate man who is honest enough and bold enough to face the really hard questions of life. He is the very son of David, now King in Jerusalem, at the height of success and fame, yet this book is saturated with words like- *futility, meaningless, no purpose, no satisfaction, useless* and *hopeless*. We walk away with a dose of reality that says the "running and the reaching", the "accruing and accomplishing", the "earning and the spending" will always leave us empty if indeed they are the priority of our pursuit. Without God in the equation nothing makes sense. He is the perspective, the foundation and the hinge- He is the reason. Without Him, none of it works.

"Oh, Lord, teach me contentment. Teach me stewardship. Help me find fulfillment. Teach me to invest my energies, talents, and passions for eternity's sake. I love You, Lord. I want to live for You."

THIRTEEN

VULTURES

"Do not be far from me, for trouble is near and there is no one to help." Psalm 22:11

"What was that? Oh, Dear Lord, what was that? What's going on...don't you want me to leave in this plane? I'm going to pass out. What is this? Help me!" I closed my eyes hoping to regain focus.

Earlier that morning I finished packing and drove 100 miles to the airport to catch this flight. I was excited about the regional meeting to be held in Salt Lake City. It was a meeting for General Managers and it was my first time to attend. I had prepared a motivational type presentation. This was important to me. It was a matter of making a good first impression. I had been so excited only moments earlier.

The flight attendant was making her final walk through, checking seats and seat belts. *Lord, if I'm supposed to get off this plane, make it clear to me; help me to know Your leading. What's wrong with me?*

Wave after wave of dizziness overtook me. I didn't know if I could actually stand up, if I could walk off the plane without help. It had come on so quickly, so out of the blue. This headache was unbearable. I had never been a "headachy" person but this was extreme pain. I was traveling with my boss. He was on my right. Our advertising director was on my left. I turned to her and asked if she had anything for a headache. She asked me if I was okay. My answer was quick, "Oh yeah, I'm fine, I just have a headache all of a sudden." I was clueless as to what was wrong but I was hopeful that it would pass quickly. I couldn't bear that either of the two people I was traveling with might know the severity of what I was feeling. As the flight attendant made a second pass I asked her for a drink so I could take the headache tablets. I took them and sat very still. I don't remember being part of the conversation during the flight. I'm sure I was because I was in the middle. I have no memory of landing at the airport or arriving at our hotel. I do remember my room. I was impressed. It was beautiful. *So this is how the other half live.*

We were on a definite schedule. We were to be treated to a trip up into the foothills to watch the Olympic contestants training for the winter sporting events. For an instant I thought of saying that I was unable to attend, but what kind of first impression would that make. I couldn't do that. I changed my clothes and met my group in the lobby. I grabbed a spot in one of the SUVs by the window. We started the trek up the mountain. I kept laying my head on the window because it was cold and I thought it would bring some relief for my headache. I hoped it would help me clear the fog, help me "snap out of it." Everything was so out of focus. Voices were magnified. The road noises were magnified. It seemed that I could hear the snow flakes as they hit the windshield. Everything was so LOUD!

We parked and everyone bolted out to walk up what I'm sure was a relatively small hill. We were being led to the side of the bob-sledding event where the Olympians were waiting for us so they could demonstrate their talent and expertise. As I looked ahead, the hill loomed over me. How would I ever make it? My vision was distorted, my breathing was labored, and my head was throbbing. I looked back at the vehicle a couple of times, thinking that I could slip back and wait there. Maybe no one would notice. About that time, someone said, "You coming?"

"Oh, yeah, I wouldn't miss it for the world." That locked me in. I had to try. *"Lord, I don't know what's going on, but please don't let me die here, don't let me die today. I'll do my best to toughen up, but please don't let me die."*

I know that it sounds like "Let's Make a Deal," but I wasn't bargaining with God. I was begging. I was so very ill. I was afraid. I thought it had to be my heart...I thought perhaps I had just had another heart attack or maybe a blood clot traveled to my head. I thought it was an aneurysm or a tumor. I thought I had contracted a horrible virus of some kind when I boarded the plane. I thought a lot of stuff. But I kept going. Somehow I found myself at the top of the hill hanging onto the side of the fence that bordered the sledding event. It was impressive. I'm sure I contributed as everyone "oohhed" and "aahhed." I was the only woman in the group and I kept thinking how noisy these men were. They were cheering, whooping and hollering. Every sound was painful.

We were led from the bobsled area to a beautiful lodge where a solid wall of windows opened to a spectacular view of the snowy hillside where Olympic skiers were practicing speed, agility, jumps, and flips. Normally I would have been out-of-my-head-excited about what I was seeing. Now however, I was just out of my head...with pain, with fear, with dread. While inside the lodge I walked away from the group twice to go into the bathroom. I was sick to my stomach and was sure I was going to vomit. I was looking for a few quiet moments, hoping to calm this storm raging inside me.

It was quite an ordeal getting all of us re-loaded in the vehicles. Finally we were back on the road and I was relieved. I thought I'd be able to go to my room and lie down until this...this... 'whatever it was' passed. About the time I was comforting myself with that thought, I heard the regional manager announce they had another surprise for us. He might have been talking at a somewhat higher volume so that everyone in the suburban could hear, but to me it sounded like he was screaming through a bull-horn. *Oh, Lord...I don't think I can make it through another event...I need to get back to my room...I don't have an option...I have no way back until the group goes back. I need a doctor..I need..I need..I need...*

We are needy people aren't we? I don't know if you are like me, but sometimes it's hard to admit that I need help. It's probably a "pride" thing. I want so much to have everything under control, to be self sufficient. Remember me, the middle child. I was truly low maintenance. I never required much attention. I'm basically an "I can manage" kind of personality. It's taken me most of my life to realize that it's okay to admit my need to God. 2 Samuel 22:7 has taught me, "In my distress I called to the Lord; I called out to my God. From his temple he heard my voice; my cry came to his ears."

Illness is always an unplanned, unwelcome inconvenience. Being away from home and not knowing exactly what was wrong or where I could turn for help added even more stress to the mix. Even though I normally have a high threshold for pain, this pain was absolutely unreal, intensified more so because I didn't know its origin. The dizziness was troublesome because I didn't know if the next wave would take me to the floor. My tunnel vision and partial vision was especially frightening because I had never experienced anything like this before. I jumped to conclusions and made uneducated guesses regarding the root cause. This was indeed despair.

Despair is never something we plan for ourselves. Looking at our crowded day-timers we would never intentionally jot down a date for 'despair'. Let's see, I need to grow...I need to mature...I have trust issues I need to work on, so let's see, on the 10th of this month I'll set aside the entire day for despair. No, crisis doesn't book appointments.

Salt Lake City is the home of a famous Pizza Parlor and our next treat was to stop there for dinner. We entered the restaurant to find that half the facility had been reserved and set up for our group. I had never been there before; I had never been to Salt Lake City before. Throughout dinner however, I kept having these surreal, out-of-body, de-ja-vu feelings. I felt as if I had been seated at this table, watched these people, and heard these conversations on some other unknown occasion. I remember how much everyone loved and enjoyed the pizza. I remember conversation and laughing. I don't think I contributed much but I did get through the meal.

I have no memory at all of getting back into the suburban or driving back to the hotel. I have no memory of getting out and walking to my room. The next thing I remember was standing outside my door and wishing I could get in. I was searching my purse for the key-card. *Oh no Lord, I'm going to have to go back down to the lobby and ask for help...Oh, Lord, I'm sick...so sick...please help me...please help me.*

After answering a message that had been left on my phone, I fell into bed. I took an Ativan, talked to the Lord a bit and fell into a deep sleep. When my alarm went off the next morning I rolled over. I don't think I moved at all throughout the night. Lying on my back and staring at the ceiling I began to take inventory. My head wasn't hurting so severely this morning. My vision seemed normal. I took my pulse. It seemed slow. I got up and walked around the room. I was weak. Looking at the clock I tried to step up my pace a little. In and out of the shower, I stood in front of the mirror. Oh, good grief...today I was going to need the entire entourage... A mess of Mabelline, more than a little L'oreal, topped off with miraculous Mary Kay...all this just to make me look alive. I'd have to settle for just looking alive because I for sure wasn't going to cross over into looking good...not today. *Thank you, Lord, I think I can make it today. I don't know why I had to get sick now, but at least I feel a little better today. Thank you. Please give me strength. Help me with my presentation. Sharpen my mind. I'm so cloudy.*

I'm sure we had a nice breakfast; I just don't remember it. I was losing blocks of time. I didn't know it then. I became aware of it later when I tried to recall the convention in its entirety. Mid morning marked the beginning of all the presentations. I was numb. I guess numb was okay...at least I wasn't nervous. There were 13 General Managers invited to speak at this conference, 12 men and me. I had put together what I believed was a stirring and inspirational topic based on how "happy employees translate into higher profits." I was well prepared and probably could have gotten through my presentation in my sleep. I barely remember my name being called; only half remember getting up and delivering my material. I must have done an okay job though because, wonder of wonders...I won. The only gal in the bunch and I won. What sweet victory. It would have been much sweeter if I could just remember it. There was a cash award for the winner and I do remember accepting the money, hearing the applause and thanking everyone.

Soon after, we were being rushed off to the airport again. To this day I can't remember being in the airport, boarding the plane, or flying home. I remember looking for my car, trying to remember where I had parked it and then driving home. I've never asked my boss if we talked during those hours. I've never admitted to him how sick I was or that I lost those hours.

The next day was Saturday. I had to be at work. We were still in the mall and Saturday was a big day. I had gotten home very late the night before. I had (the Lord only knows how) driven over 100 miles from the airport to my home. I was tired and weak when I awoke. I called in to let my staff know that I would be in after lunch. That gave me a couple of hours. I lay back down. The room was spinning. Wow, I felt really sick......

Several days later, I finally sat in the doctor's office waiting to be seen. I had postponed this office visit hoping that things would improve. The "ole' silver lining gal" was waiting for this to pass. I kept putting off going to the doctor because I believed he would just write me a prescription and send me on my way. Now, to make matters worse, my doctor was out. I was sitting here waiting for a man I had never met before. I could see what was coming...he didn't know me, he would patronize me a little...he would write me a prescription and deliver the "call if you're not better in the morning" speech. I wasn't his patient. He wasn't going to go out on a limb here.

After introductions, I began to describe my headache, the dizziness that would come and go, the magnification of sound and the funny taste in my mouth. He asked me if I was still on Coumadin, the blood thinner that had been prescribed after my heart attack and asked when the levels had last been checked. I was still on Coumadin and the levels had been checked recently. He left the room for a few minutes and came back in with my pro-time chart. "Well, Nancy, your INR is within acceptable limits. Even so, I think we need to get you over to the hospital for a CAT scan." *Oh, man, I am due back at the mall. I have customers coming in and I have a radio commercial to cut in the afternoon.* He continued, "I've called over and they're expecting you. Who brought you in today?"

"Uh, I brought myself."

"Oh, well I'll call for an ambulance to take you over."

Taken off guard, I was a little slow on the uptake but eventually managed to jump into action, "Oh, that's not necessary...I can drive myself, it's so close." After hesitating briefly, he agreed, giving further instructions for me to go straight to the hospital because the staff would be waiting for me.

I had expected the brush off, now I was on my way to the hospital for a CAT scan. I'm usually good at reading situations and people, but my instinctive skills were way off on this one. This man was being pretty cautious, almost too attentive. He had been right, however, about the hospital staff. They were waiting. The test was quick. It was painless. It was over. After the slow progression out of the cylinder I started to rise up. I had things to do, places to go. A hand was on my right shoulder. *Oh, maybe we aren't done.* Now there was a hand on my left side. Looking from my right to my left I spotted a wheel chair at my feet. *What's wrong...what's going on?*

"Nancy, you have a brain hemorrhage. We're going to take you up to the ICU." I heard it...it just didn't sink in.

"I'm being admitted?"

"Yes."

I finally made my mouth work, "I need my purse; I need my phone."

"Let's get you upstairs first, Nancy." Hey, they wouldn't give me my purse, my phone...this must be serious. "What did you say? Where am I going?" I couldn't see the nurse pushing my chair. She spoke softly into my right ear.

"You have a cerebral hemorrhage. We're taking you up to the Intensive Care Unit."

I remember watching old westerns with my dad. After valiant battles, courageous efforts, almost super-human victories, some of the cowboys would catch a wave of just plain bad luck and when they were left alone, wounded and helpless, the vultures would move in. Flying overhead, they seemed to be taunting, leering, and impatient.

They seemed to be saying, "Just give it up. Die already... Just die."

The vultures were overhead. I had been through a heart attack and I had lived through it. I had almost died because of complete lung and heart failure. My heart had been critically damaged and I had come through to the other side of that mountain with a miraculous healing. Now a year later here I was on my way to ICU with a life threatening Cerebral Hemorrhage. I was feeling battered and broken. The solemn attitude of the staff set the stage. I could tell they saw the vultures too.

Near death once again, I could feel the vultures flying in circles above me, just waiting, watching. Surrounded by their ugly blackness, I felt a small twinge of surrender. I was tired, lifeless almost, facing insurmountable odds. Where would I find the strength to fight another battle?

A Little Deeper

Has adversity beaten you down? Are you familiar with surrender?

Mark 4:35-41 is captured in my Bible with a heading entitled, "Jesus Calms The Storm". It tells the story of Jesus and His disciples together in a boat headed across a lake at the end of a long and tiring day. Verse 37 says, "A furious squall came up and the waves broke over the boat, so that it was nearly swamped." Jesus was in the stern sleeping on a cushion. The disciples woke him and said, "Teacher don't you care if we drown?" I love the rest of the story. Verse 39 says, "He got up, rebuked the wind and said to the waves, "Quiet! Be still!" Then the wind died down and it was completely calm. He said to his disciples, "Why are you so afraid? Do you still have no faith?"

The disciples were hand picked by Jesus. They traveled with him, worked with him, ate with him, prayed with him. They were right there with Jesus in Mark, Chapter 1, when he healed the man with leprosy. They had seen the paralytic lowered down, through a roof and healed by Jesus in Mark, Chapter 2. They were present as Jesus taught the crowds. Even so, they still must have had some doubt about whether Jesus was indeed the only begotten Son of God. The very question they posed, "Teacher, don't you care if we drown?" says volumes. They weren't asking for Him to do something; they were only amazed that he could sleep through the storm. Did the winds come in order to give the Lord a chance to chase away that remaining uncertainty? I have to believe if there was even an ounce of skepticism among this group, it was eradicated once and for all that very night. Verse 41 says, "They were terrified and asked each other, "Who is this? Even the wind and the waves obey Him."

I had already been through so much. Jesus had proved Himself to me over and over again, yet here I was, in the middle of yet another squall. Did my momentary feelings of surrender give my Lord cause to ask me the same question, "Why are you so afraid? Do you still have no faith?"

"Oh Lord Jesus, You are my Rock. Your works are perfect. Your ways are just. You are a faithful God who does no wrong. You are just and upright. (Deut 32:4). Increase my faith. Help me to stand firm, be strong and courageous. (I Cor 16:13)"

FOURTEEN

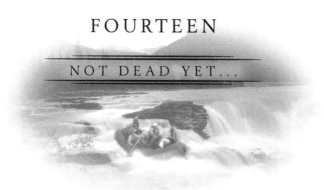

NOT DEAD YET...

"Wait for the Lord; be strong and take heart
and wait for the Lord." Psalm 27:14

I believe that everyone, at some point in his or her life, has felt the circling of the vultures. Have you had times when you've cried out, "NO, I"M NOT DEAD YET!" Possibly your vultures aren't waiting for your physical death. Maybe they're circling to watch and wait for the demise of your emotional, financial, or spiritual well being. Perhaps you're exhausted from the battle you're waging against the vultures of unbelief. When the hard times come and keep coming, it's often difficult to hang on to our beliefs. We feel forsaken by the Lord. We feel that He's absent, that He's not looking; that He's stopped caring and working on our behalf. It's hard to trust that God is doing a good work in our lives.

It seems that so many people today choose to believe in God, sing His praises, give Him glory, as long as He answers their prayers as THEY see fit. As long as the storms of life pass by leaving them only a bit damp and disheveled, as long as it's raining hardest on the surrounding areas, then their faith remains intact. I've been there.

Praise from the mountaintop is easy. Praise that reaches up from the valley is the true measure of our faith.

Remember the familiar story of Shadrach, Meshach, and Abednego? These three young men were uprooted, taken captive, and forced to live in Babylon after Jerusalem had been destroyed. King Nebuchadnezzar, took his pick of the spoil of the city of Jerusalem. The spoil included young men like Shadrach, Meshach, and Abednego. They were hand picked because they were strong and because they were young. Nebuchadnezzar hoped to be able to brain-wash them, change their thinking, eradicate their faith in God Jehovah, and eventually train them to be, not only good citizens of Babylon, but valuable advocates and assets within his service. After several years in captivity, King Nebuchadnezzar took notice of these three young men (Daniel 2:49) and promoted them to serve as administrators over the province of Babylon. This well-deserved season of their lives was threatened, however, by jealous accusers in verse 8 of chapter 3. Because Shadrach, Meshach, and Abednego were bold enough to stand up for what they believed, they stood out as being different. They found themselves in a position of grave danger when they refused to bow down before the image of gold set up by King Nebuchadnezzar. I'm drawn to their response when Nebuchadnezzar tells them they will most assuredly be thrown into a blazing furnace if they don't bow down.

He asks them, "What God will be able to rescue you?" I love it when they answer in verse 17, "The God we serve is able to save us." Those few words say it all. They were walking the talk...living out their steadfast, unconditional belief, their trust and faith in God Almighty. Their response goes on in verse 18 with the words, "But even if He does not, we will worship Him anyway." There it is...I know without a doubt He has the power to deliver me from harm, from hard times, of any kind. But even if He does not...I will worship and praise Him anyway.

I don't want mine to be a 911 kind of faith. I don't want my connection with God to be initiated by emergency or crisis. I don't want to have to dial up, be connected or re-connected. I want a REAL relationship with my Lord. I want my own dedicated line, one that's always open, frequently used throughout each and every day and night, and one that never disconnects. My Lord offers me that kind of access. What a privilege to have a private line, a personal link, an audience with the King of Kings and Lord of Lords!

Within His divine plan and wisdom, He may not bring healing and resolve to every situation, but I want to be so closely connected with Him that it's easy for me to say, "even if He does not, I will worship Him anyway.

Trying desperately to get my mind around what was happening to me, I mentally quoted scripture. In my mind I began to recall lines of worship songs and hymns; I rehearsed the miracle stories in the Bible. Knowing that there was bleeding going on in my brain, I believed it was crucial I stay focused. I didn't want to lose reality. So I concentrated...I worked hard at consciousness. What I knew best and what I needed most centered on God's Word, His love and His promises.

Romans chapter 4 tells us the story of Abraham. Beginning in verse 18 the story recounts, "Against all hope, Abraham in hope believed...Without weakening in his faith, he faced the fact that his body was as good as dead, since he was about a hundred years old...and that Sarah's womb was also dead." When Abraham was over 100 years old, God told him he was going to be a daddy. I'm afraid my response might have been sarcastic, skeptical...my voice saturated with disbelief and hurt. But not Abraham...read on.

"Yet (the "yet" pointing out this was an impossible, unheard of notion, contrary to logic and common sense, but even so...) he did not waver through unbelief regarding the promise of God, but was strengthened in his faith and gave glory to God...being fully persuaded that God had power to do what he had promised." Abraham didn't succumb to doubt. God said it and he believed it. What a simple concept. Why do we allow our doubt to complicate the issue?

I love these heroes of the Scripture. I try to grab on to and emulate their spirit and example. In the early stages, the shock of hearing about the brain hemorrhage initiated a bout of discouragement, a time of dealing with trust issues. I was for a time overwhelmed with the doubt and fear running around in my head. I was allowing myself to watch the vultures. Having been made aware of the seriousness of the situation, my hope was looking pretty dead. When hope dies, all signs of life are gone and the vultures move in. Yet, having put to memory verses like Hebrews 13:5 "Never will I leave you, never will I forsake you," I was able to find the strength to wave them off.

I'm not sure that on this particular day, facing this particular onslaught, that my thoughts were formulated. I'm not sure there was really any semblance of order with regard to what was going through my mind. I am sure I was wondering, *Why? Why me? Why now? Haven't I been through enough?* I'm thankful I was able to face this valley with the conviction that even though I didn't understand it..even though I was petrified with fear, I did know that God was in control. I loved and trusted Him...no matter what.

I was settled into the ICU room. After changing into a hospital gown and after getting three intravenous lines started, I had a moment to catch my breath. I tried to regroup. My life was in a tail-spin...again...but I still had choices. Although everything happening to me was seemingly unfair and untimely, I did have control over one thing. With God's help, I could control my response. Circumstances were what they were...my reaction was what would make the situation a victory or a tragedy. I could choose to believe the worst and succumb to the vultures. Or I could choose to believe God, trust God, and praise God, no matter what. Including my mishap on the Poudre River I had been faced with death four times within the last year and a half. In each of those situations God had been there. He had lifted me, encouraged me, and healed me. To give into the feelings of being forsaken now, when God had saved me countless times up to this point would have been fickle and immature. I needed to remain faithful.

There was so much activity in the room. Even though my concentration was fierce, I know my prayers were snatches, disjointed, disheveled, and way short of eloquent. Even so I know they were heard. I know the Lord was there.

My cardiologist ran from his previous emergency to mine. He reiterated that I had a hemorrhage. There was considerable swelling that was causing the brain stem to shift. He was encouraged that I was not only conscious at this point but aware and coherent. He had already called a neurosurgeon. When he arrived they put their heads together and presented me with three plans of attack. First, I was informed they could do a surgical procedure. They could make an incision just behind my right ear, go in and clean up the hemorrhage like an oil spill. Secondly, they could go in with a needle and try to drain it. The third option was to wait. I asked about the risk factors and was told that all three options had relatively the same risks; death, seizures, paralysis, long term damage that could affect my speech and mobility.

The prayers for help were being fired off in my brain. I never laid down the phone. I kept God on the line, begging Him for wisdom and direction. It didn't feel right, but both doctors, both specialists, were asking me for a decision. I had to call it. I decided on the third option; I decided to be still, wait and see. I remember the over-whelming presence of God in that room on that day. He gave me such peace. At a time when instinct was telling all of us to take action, take control, and do what we could do to turn this thing around, my Lord was saying wait. We were hoping that if we discontinued the blood thin-ner, administered frozen blood plasma, vitamin K and ste-roids, the bleeding would stop. If it did, then there was a chance, slim though it was, that the hemorrhage would heal like a bruise. The best-case scenario would be that the blood in my brain would be absorbed and the swelling would diminish. The neurosurgeon said that because I was conscious and aware, he was willing to take a "wait and see" approach but only for the next 24 hours. They would watch me carefully, do an MRI the next evening to make sure that things hadn't worsened. If there was no improvement, we would proceed with surgery.

A Little Deeper

Have you ever faced death? Have you ever had to make a life and death decision for yourself or for a loved one? Did you have a peace that you were doing the right thing?

I've heard people say when they are giving account of such situations that they had no where to turn, but to God. Think of a time you "turned to God." What road were you traveling before you became aware the turn was necessary? Describe how you made that turn?

Consider these verses:

Isaiah 30:21   Psalm 26:3   Psalm 89:15
Psalm 128:1   Deut 5:33

"Oh, Lord Jesus, help me to 'walk' closely with you, in tune with your leading, in step with your direction. I pray that my relationship with you will be real, alive and active. I love You, Lord."

FIFTEEN

I NEED A SIGN

"Listen to My voice, and do according to all which I command you; so you shall be my people, and I will be your God." Jeremiah 11:4

I often find myself praying that God will give me a sign; show me the answer, the direction. If I just had a sign it would make everything so much easier. If I had a sign, a clear, unquestionable happening, then I could hang out that "now I know what God wants me to do" shingle and forge ahead full steam, without doubt, confusion, or fear.

I cherish the story of a widow in I Kings 17. God told Elijah to go to Zarephath of Sidon and stay there. He said that there would be a widow there who would supply Elijah with food. In fact, God tells Elijah in verse 8 that He has paved the way by commanding the widow to make sure Elijah has food. We don't know the widow's name. We only know that God spoke to her, commanded her. We find in verse 12 that the widow was tentative and understandably so. There was a drought in the land. These were hard times. Stepping out with this kind of blind faith was not an easy assignment. When Elijah asked her for a drink and for some food she said, "I don't have any bread, only a handful of flour in a jar and a little oil in a jug. I am gathering a few sticks to take home and make a meal for myself and my son, that we may eat it and die." I identify with this sweet woman. God commanded her. He made it clear He had a purpose for her, yet she was at war with the logical. She was a mom. She understood the facts at hand. She had a son to think about.

Elijah tells her in verse 13, "Don't be afraid. Go home and do as you have said, but first make a small cake of bread for me from what you have and bring it to me, and then make something for yourself and your son. For this is what the Lord, the God of Israel, says: "The jar of flour will not be used up and the jug of oil will not run dry until the day the Lord gives rain on the land." Verse 15 tells us that despite her logic, she did what God and Elijah encouraged her to do. Please take note that she didn't know Elijah. She had never laid eyes on him before. Consider for a moment how we react to strangers in general, and how magnified our reaction would be if a stranger asked us for a seemingly impossible favor.

What would we have done in her shoes, especially when what he was asking her to do was in essence taking the food right out of her son's mouth? The Bible says that at this point she stepped out, more than likely still very uneasy and unsure. However, she was richly rewarded for her step of faith. As the days passed the miracle of the un-empty jars greeted her every morning. Verse 26 tells us, "For the jar of flour was not used up and the jug of oil did not run dry, in keeping with the word of the Lord spoken by Elijah."

She had her sign. It wasn't just a quick, lightening

bolt in the sky kind of one time happening, it was a daily miracle that she witnessed and absolutely appreciated and benefited from day in and day out. But look at the verses that follow. Verse 17 says that sometime later her son became ill. Here it is, the absolute worst nightmare a mother could imagine. Her faith is shaken; she begins to doubt. Her doubt bounces around in my head.

Maybe taking this man in wasn't a God-thing. Who am I that I would hear the voice of God and know His will? Maybe God is angry with me. Maybe God is punishing me. Maybe it's all just a gimmick..... a sick joke..... what if there is no God?"

The questions come, don't they? At some point in life the questions come. We all deal with doubt. There's really no point in hiding it. Honest people deal with doubt. Even the giants of the faith deal with doubt.

In verse 18, the widow lashes out and accuses Elijah. "What do you have against me, man of God? Did you come to remind me of my sin and kill my son?" Her torment was tremendous. Her doubt was on a rampage. Elijah says in verse 19, "Give me your son." In the midst of her grief and confusion she doesn't know what else to do. Evidently permission was given, because verse 18 says that Elijah took the widow's son to the upper room that had been his quarters.

"O Lord my God, have you brought tragedy also upon this widow I am staying with, by causing her son to die?" And now the doubt has spread to Elijah. (I've been there. My suffering is one thing, but why do my loved ones have to suffer alongside me?) God's word tells us that Elijah stretched himself over the boy three times, petitioning God, "O Lord my God, let this boy's life return to him!" Verse 22 says, "The Lord heard Elijah's cry, and the boy's life returned to him, and he lived." This is the very first account given of a resurrection miracle. Elijah handed the boy back to his mother and said, "Look, your son is alive!"

Don't miss this now....the woman replies, "Now I KNOW that you are a man of God and that the word of the Lord from your mouth is the truth." See the merciful affirmation of God. He gave her clarity. He had already rewarded her initial step of faith back when she gave all she had to Elijah. And He continues to honor her obedience with an unprecedented miracle. Bless her heart. She had some trying times. She dealt with a lot of grey area along the way. I can just see her walking over to the jars every day, wondering if this morning would be the morning that she would find them empty. Then her son becomes ill and he actually dies. Things don't get much worse than that. But here she is at the end of the road. The last we hear of her is when she makes the statement, "NOW I KNOW!"

Sometimes God gives us a sign. Certainly He has the power to prove Himself to us in lightening bolt fashion day in and day out, but I have come to realize that God isn't in the proving business. He is God; He doesn't have to prove anything. He's in the faith business. Proof is less important than relationship. Oh, that I would learn to be steadfast in my faith, believing who God is, never losing sight of His power and might, walking closely with Him, knowing without a doubt that my best is what He has in mind for me.

The next 24 hours in the Intensive Care Unit were the longest of my life. If I ever needed a sign, I needed it then. I was in a great deal of pain, and terribly nauseated by the pain medication. I had several intravenous tubes running. I didn't sleep. My vision was blurry so I couldn't read. There are no TVs in intensive care and visitors are restricted. The steroids made me feel like I could absolutely leap that five-story hospital building in one single bound. The clock didn't seem to move at all. It was so hard to be still and quiet. I prayed. I recited verses in my head. I sang; very, very quietly, but I sang.

Initially I felt so sure it had been God's leading to wait instead of rush in to surgery. I truly felt His presence giving me peace about the decision at the time, but now, only hours later, I was afraid. The "what-ifs?" began to take over. The guessing, the imagining, the fears were all screaming in my ear. The neurosurgeon told me it was lucky I had decided to see about the headache when I did because the swelling had begun to shift the brain stem. If I had continued to take the daily prescription of blood thinner, I probably would have been dead within days. I knew... without a shadow of a doubt...I KNEW it wasn't luck...it was God. It wasn't coincidental I sought help just in time. God prompted me, urged me, led me. Even so, now the doubt was creeping in.

I was like the widow. I can see her walking to the jars every morning. She was wondering if the promise of God, the grace of God was real. Would it last; would it carry her through yet another day? I lay in the Intensive Care Unit and as the hours crept slowly by I was overwhelmed by all the same emotions. I was so afraid. I was wondering.

A Little Deeper

We are desperate for the signs, the miracles, the fixes, the answers. But the Lord asks us to step out in faith, faith alone.
Consider Hebrews 11. Verse 1 says:

"Now faith is being sure of what we hope for and certain of what we do not see."

This famous "By Faith" chapter recalls 15 giants of the faith, heroes and heroines alike...from Abraham to Moses, to Noah, to Rahab. They are all being remembered and commended for stepping out in faith, faith alone.

"Father, help me to search Your Word, to know Your heart. When my fear demands a sign, cover me with Your love, Your comfort and Your courage. Help me fix my eyes on You alone, the author and finisher of my faith."

SIXTEEN

AFFIRMATION

"But I trust in you, O Lord; I say, "You are my God.
My times are in your hands..."
Psalm 31: 14,15

"Good morning, Nancy. How's it going?" The neurosurgeon was in early the next day.

"I feel really jumpy."

He shook his head as if agreeing, "Yeah, that's the steroids. How's your headache?"

"It's bad, it's really bad."

He asked me about my vision. He did some reflex and balance type tests and told me that we would be doing the MRI early that afternoon. *Oh, we're not going to wait the full 24 hours like we talked about yesterday? What's up? What's wrong? What does he see?* I didn't ask any of these questions aloud. I kept them to myself. I shook my head in agreement and he was gone.

The MRI equipment at the hospital was down and I had to be taken by ambulance to another location. One of the ICU nurses went with me. I'm a little claustrophobic but on a good day I can get my "mind over matter" and handle an MRI. This wasn't a good day. I was a mess. I know the steroids played a big role in the anxiety I was feeling. I knew it then. It just didn't help to know it. The test took about an hour and a half but it seemed an eternity. I kept trying to focus on the words of a song by Ron Hamilton that I had learned years ago.

"God NEVER MOVES WITHOUT PURPOSE OR PLAN.
WHEN TRYING A SERVANT OR MOLDING A MAN.
GIVE THANKS TO THE LORD THOUGH YOUR TESTING SEEMS LONG.
IN DARKNESS HE GIVETH A SONG.
OH, REJOICE IN THE LORD. HE MAKES NO MISTAKE.
HE KNOWETH THE END OF EACH PATH THAT I TAKE.
FOR WHEN I AM TRIED AND CRUCIFIED, I SHALL COME FORTH AS GOLD."

I sang the song over and over again in my head. I believed it. I cherished its truth.

Oh thank you Lord, its over. Thank you...Thank you. We were on our way back to the hospital. It was too early for pain medication when we left but now it was overdue. The knocking and pounding of the MRI machine was deafening. I was in a great deal of pain. The nurse called ahead and they had a shot waiting for me when we got back.

Being back in my room brought some relief. I would try to settle down and deal with the pain. I would try to be still and let the medication do its work. Now the waiting would begin. I was out-of-my-mind miserable for the next few hours, watching for the doctor, waiting for the answers.

"Hello. Sorry they had to take you downtown. How was the trip?" He was talking and reading my chart at the same time.

"Ok I guess. Do we know anything yet?" Usually I enjoy and even initiate small talk but I was ready to get on with it. I was praying for good news, trying to prepare myself in case of bad.

"Well, it doesn't look like things have worsened. The area isn't larger and hopefully that means the bleeding has stopped." *Praise God..Praise God!* He went on to say that there was still considerable concern about the shifting of the brain stem. He told me to be quiet and try to sleep, in fact he ordered something to make me sleep, and said that he would see me the following day.

I fought closing my eyes. Everyone had been so impressed with my consciousness, my alertness, I hated to surrender it. But the sleeping pill won. When I opened my eyes, Mandy was there. I'm not sure how long she had been there but it was good to see her. She told me she had just sent three of my staff members away because the nurses wanted me to sleep. I was surprisingly okay with that. I had slept, evidently throughout the night, but even so, I felt exhausted. I reasoned that it was probably the after effects of the sedatives. I cat napped throughout the morning and waited for the doctor to come back in.

This was day 3 in the intensive care unit. My cardiologist came in during the lunch hour. He was glad to report that my heart had been behaving itself. I was hooked up to the monitors and they had been watching it on a regular basis. He explained to me that there was a relatively high risk of my having seizure activity and if it weren't for my heart problem they would have already started to give me anti-seizure medication. Evidently the medicine I was taking to keep my heart in rhythm could not be taken along with the seizure medication. We dodged the medication dilemma for the time being. This would definitely have been a tough call to make and I don't think either one of us had the energy at that point to deal with it.

Toward evening, the neurosurgeon was back. He repeated the information about the conflict of seizure medication. He said he was confident that we would need to address the situation, if not now, down the road during my healing process. I latched on to the words, *"healing process."* "So, what I hear you saying is, I am healing." I made it a statement not a question.

"No, I don't believe healing has begun at this point, but it appears that the bleeding has stopped. The next week or so we hope to see signs that the blood in your brain is diminishing, being absorbed. When we see the size of the area actually shrink, then I'll be ready to say you're healing." He rushed on, "Nancy, I know you want a time frame here. Let me just say you're a lucky, lucky lady, but the road to full recovery is going to be a long one. I'm talking at least six months here." He read the questions on my face and did his best to cover all the bases. He explained I would be in the hospital for quite some time and the healing process we were all hoping for would be very, very slow. He took a moment before he left to talk to me about how fortunate I was just to be alive. He talked about how encouraging it was to watch a miracle unfold and how humbling it was to realize that 'Someone" bigger than all of us was in charge.

As the days stretched on, I was given a little more freedom. On about day eight, I was allowed to sit up in a chair. A day or so later I was allowed to walk around in the hall. I can remember the staff watching me as if I were some kind of freak. One of the nurses mentioned that it was really out of the norm to have a patient in Intensive Care walking around the halls and she just wasn't comfortable with it. I tried not to walk past her after that. I didn't want her to be uncomfortable.

I began to talk to the doctors about going home. They ordered another MRI and a brain wave test. The swelling was down somewhat and there was no sign of anything misfiring in my brain, so at the end of two weeks I was on my way home. It was a Thursday afternoon when Mandy got me settled into my own bedroom.

The following Monday morning I was back at work. I didn't ask the doctors about going back. I wasn't sure if I would have had their blessing or not. One thing I was sure of was that my employers couldn't hold my job for six months. I hoped and prayed that this healing process would happen as I continued to work.

True to prediction, the road ahead was rough. I had an on-going headache. I went to bed at night with an ice pack in one hand and a heating pad in the other. There were several occasions when I became violently ill. I experienced nausea, vomiting, dizziness, and vision problems. Even so, I was driven, obsessed with a sense of "beating this thing"...getting completely well. I felt an uncommon, probably unhealthy determination to push myself.

Three months later, I had another MRI. They gave me the exact measurements of the hemorrhage at the onset and quoted the size of it now, three months later. All I really heard was that it was smaller than before. *Praise God!* Five months down the road, another MRI revealed that the hemorrhage was the size of a fingernail. Originally, it had been the size of a closed fist. This was good.

This was HOPE.

In May of that year, construction was completed on the new Saturn facility. There was much to do. In June we had our Grand Opening. For months I felt half-mast on the inside, but I made sure the flag was flying high relative to my performance. I worked very hard at staying focused and attending to detail. No one knew what I was going through and when asked about the hemorrhage I always threw out positive responses. I was happy with myself for being able to, despite the grave circumstances, perform at an optimum level. It would have been easier to have had a job where I could have just clocked in and shown up. During the healing months after the onset of the cerebral hemorrhage, however, I had to be visionary, excited, and enthusiastic. I couldn't let down for a minute. I faked a lot of things but I couldn't fake the spirit that was required to build a strong team and get a new business off the ground. I know it was only God's grace that carried me through. My prayer journals from that period of time are marked with tears. I pleaded with God on a daily basis. I begged Him for the chance to be whole again, completely well and whole.

I saw several neurosurgeons during those months and they were all astounded with my progress and recovery. I had countless opportunities to give God praise. Once again, the Lord had rescued me from a situation that should have demanded my life. He heard my cry. He answered my prayers. He upheld me and healed me.

By the end of July I was beginning to feel better, really better. I, of course, had been taken off the blood thinning medication, so now I faced a relatively high risk of developing a blood clot if I were to have an A-fib episode. The good news was that I was still taking the Cordarone and it was keeping the episodes at bay. Another piece of good news was that I never had to face making a decision about the anti-seizure medication. To the best of my knowledge I never had a full seizure. I had been told to prepare for them. I had been told they were inevitable. I had at least four months filled with pre-seizure auras. But the seizures never came. *Praise God!*

I buried myself in my job. I felt good about my performance. I was proud of our team and proud of our accomplishments. My excitement was building because now, six months down the road, I was beginning to feel physically well enough to tackle the vision I had cast not only for myself but for the business as a whole.

A Little Deeper

1 Corinthians 2:5 reminds us that our faith should not rest on man's wisdom, but on God's power. In the midst of turmoil, resting is never easy. Our instinct is to act...to do something. But if we will just keep focused on God's power as we walk through the valley, He will provide the calming affirmation that we need along the way.

As I write this section of the book , its Christmas time and I'm reminded that even though The Old Testament proclaimed the coming of the Messiah, when Jesus was born he was recognized by few. I think it's crucial to note that most "church people" didn't recognize Him. He didn't fit their blueprint. He wasn't what they had in mind. He didn't come packaged according to their specifications and certainly

His lowly form of arrival didn't meet up to their standards. God sent His Son in a time, in a way, to a people, that fit what He had in mind to do. As we walk close to Him, He will not only direct our path and keep us on course, He will lovingly affirm the direction along the way. His affirmation comes to us in His way and in His timing. Our job is to watch for it and recognize it.

Recall a storm in your life, a time of great pain, fear, and confusion...a time when you were desperate for a sign, waiting for an answer. Did you rest on the promises and power of God? Did you receive divine affirmation along the way? Were you able to look back and see the entire situation solved and sealed with the fingerprints of God. How did it humble you? How did it strengthen your faith?

The following Scriptures give us insight and inspiration as we see affirmation given to God's people:

Joseph...Genesis 45:4-5

Moses...Exodus 3:2-4

The Israelites...Exodus 13:21-22

Joshua's...Joshua 6:20

David...I Samuel 17:50

John the Baptist...John 3:13

Paul...Acts 16:25-26

"Precious Lord, keep me close to Your side. I want to walk in Your paths. I seek Your direction. I pray You will give me understanding and wisdom from on high. I pray you will send peace and assurance along the way. Help me to realize that Your plan for my life comes with a rainbow of hope."

SEVENTEEN

THE AIR I BREATHE

"I am the vine; you are the branches. If a man remains in me
and I in him, he will bear much fruit;
apart from me you can do nothing."
John 15:5

My health, my strength, and my performance were
exemplary for the next year and a half. I found my stride.
I was a good leader, full of enthusiasm and inspiration. I
nurtured trust within our organization. I led with honesty, sacrifice and love. The end result was not only a
successful bottom line but a family of employees who took
ownership of the overall vision.

God answered my prayer. He healed the bleeding in
my brain. It left a scar and I was warned about possible
future problems, but I didn't dwell on that. Six months
down the road I felt well and I woke up every morning
praising God for being whole again. The Cordarone was
an absolute miracle drug and my heart problem was being
managed better than ever before. I found my stride within
the business world. The company was exceeding projections and life was good. I was at ease with myself and my
performance. For this short period of time I felt like I was

actually on a level playing field. Every day I charged out of the gate without a handicap and it felt good.

In early December the receptionist buzzed me to let me know my doctor's office was on the line. I had actually made it in to see her a week or so earlier for a general physical. I picked up the phone quickly, not wanting to take too much of her time. "Hello."

"Hello, Nancy, this is Dr. Guidry."

"Yes," I said, "Thank you for calling."

"Oh, you're welcome. I just wanted you to know that all your test results are back on my desk today and most everything looks good." I didn't miss her carefully chosen words, "most everything." She went on to tell me that my red blood cell count was low and she needed me to come back in to have it rechecked. I was impressed with her thoroughness and made a note on my calendar to get back in for another blood test. A funny thing happens in the mind of someone dealing with chronic illness. Over the years I had gotten into the habit of tuning out all the 'small stuff'. I surmised that this information fell into the 'small stuff' category and quickly filed it in the non-priority box. My gynecologist was just being cautious and I was thankful for her dedication.

It actually took me a couple of weeks to find the time to run back to the Lab. I heard from my Doctor a couple of days after that. Relative to the red blood cell count, the second test confirmed the findings of the first. In the weeks that followed I had a colonoscopy, an endoscopy and a CAT scan. The search was on; she was looking for internal bleeding. My blood count was low and it appeared that I was losing blood. The next time my doctor called she reported finding something of concern. The

CAT scan had been done in an effort to rule out possible problems with internal organs and none were found. A shadow, however, showed up in the spinal area and my doctor referred me to a neurosurgeon.

Accompanied by a giant anxiety attack, I found myself sitting in the same waiting room, scheduled to see the same neurosurgeon that had taken care of me when I had the hemorrhage. When he came in he assumed I was there for a follow-up visit. Surprised to hear about the new issue, he reviewed the letter and the scan and sent me to have an MRI. I thought this was a real bother...I was a busy lady. I didn't have time for this. Much to my surprise, the MRI revealed serious stenosis in the upper spinal column aggravated by a tumor that had attached itself to the outer spine. The problem was evidently serious enough that it was interrupting my production of red blood cells. It was also the reason for some pretty severe back pain I had been experiencing. He discovered it at a critical point, just before it interfered with bowel and bladder control. There was definitely opportunity for praise in all this; I just had a hard time finding it in the maze.

The neurosurgeon recommended I have surgery as soon as possible. I did my best to maintain composure and tried to take control of the situation. I told him I would make some arrangements and get back to him to schedule a time. He grabbed the control away from me and insisted we do it as soon as we could clear a surgical room at the hospital.

I worried about cancer. I worried about the surgery paralyzing me. I worried about how long I would be down. I worried about my Atrial Fibrillation. I made sure the surgeon and the anesthesiologist knew about my heart and what medication I was on.

I was being rolled into surgery less than a week later. It was a blessing I didn't have too much time to think about what was ahead. If I had known the extent of the surgery, the pain involved, or the circumstances that would surround my recovery, the fear would have devastated me.

I told the anesthesiologist that I had a lot of anxiety about lying on my stomach. He agreed I would be asleep before they rolled me over. I prayed all the way to the operating room that he would remember his promise. He did. I went under on my back and woke up on my back. *Thank you, Lord.*

Having had several surgeries, I thought I knew what to expect. I recognized the recovery room and I was thankful it was over. I volleyed between sleep and almost sleep for quite some time. I could feel the blood pressure cuff. That was normal. I was hooked up to oxygen. I reasoned that was probably normal as well. At some point, as I phased in and out, I thought I felt something on my chest. I didn't have the strength to raise my hand to investigate. I woke again as I was being transported to my room. My family pooled into the elevator and gathered around my bedside. I began to tell them everything was okay. Everything went well. I didn't really have any basis for that kind of proclamation, but I was awake, I was aware, so everything must be okay.

Their responses seemed less than enthusiastic or maybe it was their lack of response, but I was too out of it to actually question it at that moment. I was comforted by the sounds of their footsteps beside me as I was being rolled down the hallway. Then I saw the doorway of the room I was being taken into. *Wait a minute...this isn't a normal hospital room...I recognize this room.* The entire front side was glass. It had a sliding glass doorway. This was intensive care. I had been here...in this very room when I had my cerebral hemorrhage. I looked up at my sister... "Why am I here?" I'm not sure she understood my question. Perhaps she was just hedging,

"You're in the hospital, Nancy. You just had surgery."

"I know," I said. "Why am I in intensive care?"

Everyone was asked to leave for a minute until I was settled in. I looked at my brother who was standing in the doorway. "Why intensive care?" I asked him. He was always straight with me. He would tell me. His eyes met mine with reassurance but before he could speak he was shooed away by the staff. I struggled to stay awake and aware. Two nurses were standing over me, untangling lines and hooking me up to monitors. I HAD felt something on my chest earlier. It was a heart monitor. "What's going on?" I asked. "Did I have a heart attack?"

"You just came from surgery, Nancy." Why was everyone repeating what I already knew? Did they think I didn't know where I had been? I wasn't that out of it...I just needed some answers. "I know, I just had back surgery, but why am I in intensive care?" The answer that came spoke of taking precautions, and watching me closely. That satisfied me for the moment.

The next time I woke up I was in such horrible pain I didn't really care what room I was in. Oh, my goodness. I wasn't prepared for this. I called for help. I was given a shot and a button to push that administered pain medication. I never let go of that little button. I wanted it in my hand and ever-ready. I was in agony.

Because I was in intensive care my visitors were restricted. My family could come in two at a time for only 10 minutes per hour. I encouraged them to go home and get some rest.

There's nothing more wearisome than holding vigil for a loved one that's just out of surgery. I felt bad that they were being put through this ordeal.

It was the next day before I got any real answers about why the decision had been made to send me to intensive care. My surgeon told me I had gone into Atrial Fibrillation during surgery and that he and the anesthesiologist had decided to set me up in the ICU so that they could monitor me for a couple of days. He said my cardiologist had been contacted and he would probably check in on me. Later that day the anesthesiologist came by to see me. He added a little more information to the mix when he told me that my oxygen levels were not good during the operation. He was concerned enough to call a pulmonary specialist and told me that I would be seeing her later that day.

I probably would have spent more time worrying, but the first few days after surgery I was in so much pain I could only summon enough focus to deal with the immediate, in-my-face dilemma. All other questions would have to wait. I did see my cardiologist and was visited by the pulmonary specialist. Their biggest concern was that I wasn't oxygenating properly.

On the fifth day I was moved from intensive care to the regular floor. At that time a physical therapist was assigned to me. I assumed he was there to help me deal with my pain level, help me work my muscles, walk with me...in general just to help me learn to physically function again. It took me by surprise when I realized he was there to hook me up to a mobile oxygen unit. I told him I didn't think I needed the oxygen anymore and I knew it was going to hurt like crazy but I would try to go for a walk in the hallway with him. He then explained to me that there would be no leaving my bed without the oxygen. I most definitely needed it, it had been ordered, and I just needed to cooperate. I hadn't meant to be uncooperative. I just didn't realize what was happening.

I've learned that acceptable oxygen levels are within a range of 90 and above. Mine were below 80. I was scheduled for a couple of tests. The first one was to rule out blood clots in my legs and lungs. I was safe on that count; there were no clots. The next was a diffusion test. I was familiar with this one. It was a test I had at least twice a year while on the Cordarone. It measured lung capacity. I didn't do so well on this one. That afternoon my cardiologist came to see me. He paid close attention to the arteries in my neck. He told me he feared I was in congestive heart failure. He apologized in advance, telling me that he was ordering Lasix to flush fluids out of my system and he knew it would probably keep me up throughout the night.

He was right; I was up..and down..and up..and down for several hours. The next day found me 10 pounds lighter. Now that should be cause for shouting hallelujahs! Before I could get too smug, however, I was being taken downstairs for more tests. I was weak and beginning to feel some rumble in my chest. *Am I going into A-fib?*

My cardiologist and the pulmonary specialist met me back in my room. It isn't often you get this much attention. I should have known this wasn't going to be good. I should have seen it coming, but I didn't. "Nancy, we need to talk to you about your lung function." My heart doctor was speaking. "Do you remember being made aware of the risk factors involved relative to taking the prescription Cordarone for your heart arrhythmia?" *No..No God...don't let them take away my medicine...I need that medicine.*

"Yeah, I remember. What's wrong?"

"The tests today show considerable damage to you lungs. We need to get you off the Cordarone."

A Little Deeper

When I tried to walk around, even in my room, without being hooked up to the oxygen, the staff would rush in and tell me that I MUST plug in. I thought I could do without the cumbersome bottle, but the nurses knew better. They insisted I be connected to the oxygen. This picture gives opportunity for a great analogy. Just as it was dangerous for me to take even a step without being connected to that source of strength found in the oxygen bottle, it is dangerous as well to take a step without being connected to Jesus, the source of all spiritual strength and well-being. A line from a worship song says it well when talking about our need of the Savior, "This is the Air I breath, I'm desperate for You...I'm lost without You."

Read:

Psalm 42:1
Psalm 63:1

"Oh Lord help me to seek You with the same desperation I have when gasping for air. Help me to thirst after You. Help me to be connected to Your strength and power. I'm desperate for You...I'm lost with You!"

EIGHTEEN

ALONE... WITHOUT HELP

"The Lord is with you, mighty warrior."
Judges 6:12

Remember Gideon? He's been labeled the reluctant leader of the Old Testament. He was chosen by God to be Commander in Chief, in charge of a great battle against the Midianites in Judges Chapter 6 and 7. He faced a tremendous amount of doubt, insecurity, and fear. He persisted in asking God for clarity and re-assurance every step of the way. I think Gideon must have felt like many of us feel when asked to do something outside of our comfort zone. I think it's important though, that we don't mistake reluctance for weakness or faithlessness. I sometimes think Gideon gets a bum rap. He is often criticized for not immediately jumping into action. He is accused of not having enough faith. I like Gideon. I admire him for doing everything possible to discern the perfect will of God. I respect him for his total reliance on God Almighty and for his desire to make sure that above all else, God was in absolute control. He doesn't get full of himself and charge ahead with his own battle plans, asking God to bless what he has in mind. After Gideon made positively sure in Chapter 6 that this calling was truly of God, he arrives on the scene in Chapter 7 with thirty-two thousand soldiers. Can't you hear him, "Here we are God, reporting for duty!" He must have been pleased with the turn out. I'm sure this mighty show of force did wonders for Gideon's confidence.

But look in Judges 7:2. The Lord said to Gideon, "You have too many men for me to deliver Midian into their hands." Whoa...how can you have too many men? Even though Gideon hadn't earned his position as 'General' of this army, I'm sure logic told him the more men you have, the better your chances for victory. In verse 3, God commands Gideon to announce, "Anyone who trembles with fear may turn back and leave." Twenty-two thousand men left, ten thousand remained. I can feel Gideon's confusion as he wonders what God is doing? Why would He leave him with only ten thousand men? I can hear him as he tried to apply reason, "Well, okay..ten thousand of the bravest men, trained and ready for battle, maybe we can still pull this thing off." But in verse 4 God tells Gideon again that he still has too many men. He lays out a plan for Gideon to trim the troops even further. In the end, only three hundred men are left to face the Midianites.

It doesn't seem like the best of battle plans does it? Verse 12 tells us that the enemy had "settled in the valley, thick as locusts. Their camels could no more be counted than the sand on the seashore." Talk about being outnumbered. It's a good thing Gideon spent so much time getting to know the heart of God. Many of us waste time complaining that we don't know God's will for our lives. We want to stumble across it in some mystical, daily horoscope-type manner, when what we really need is to spend time getting to know God better, developing a real and consistent relationship with Him. God wants us to lean into this relationship with Him. He wants us to trust Him, follow Him, and step by step learn to, without question or hesitation, obey His leading. It's not easy to relinquish our trust and obedience and certainly we can't hand over the reigns until and unless we've spent time getting to know the Source of our Hope.

The Bible doesn't say Gideon understood God's plan. But he was at the ever-ready, waiting for the next divine instruction. God suggested that Gideon go down and spy on the enemy camp and listen to what they were saying. He heard the enemy talking about an interpretation of a dream. He came away encouraged and re-committed. He didn't know how all this was going to work. He couldn't begin to fathom what would take place.

But even without understanding, Gideon obeyed God. He was able to move forward because now he knew God, he had spent time with God, and he trusted God without reservation. Armed with that trust, three hundred faithful warriors, trumpets, torches, and jars, he stepped into the battle. Against all odds, the victory belonged to Israel. They didn't have the largest army. They didn't have the greatest weapons, or the best resources, but they won the battle.

TO GOD BE THE GLORY!

I certainly didn't understand what was happening in my life. I had questions. I was scared to death. Without the medication how was I going to function? Even though the Cordarone had kept my arrhythmias at bay for almost three years, it had now become evident it was damaging my lungs and perhaps even my liver. I knew about the warnings. It had been made clear to me this was a 'last resort' medication and these were possible side effects but it was also pointed out that they were rare. The small dosage I was on presented only one chance in a thousand for these specific problems to arise. Here I was...dutifully showing up as the ONE in that thousand to solidify this tragic statistic.

We were backed into a corner, left only with choosing the lesser of two evils. It seemed to me at the time a choice of how to die. Certainly I didn't want to die of lung failure. I could only imagine what it would be like to have my lungs shut down. My aunt cared for her sister during the last years of her life and watched her agonizing death brought on by fibrosis of the lungs. It was horrifying. We needed to do whatever necessary to try to stop the process of the failure and resulting fibrosis in my lungs. It was our hope that the present lung dysfunction would improve after discontinuing the medication. But what was to become of me? Left with no medication to help with my Atrial Fibrillation and no blood thinner to protect against clots, I was now going to be catapulted to the top of the high risk heart patient list again, inevitably lumped into yet another tragic and possibly deadly statistic. With nothing to hold the episodes of arrhythmia at bay, I would surely fall back into having episodes several times a week. I knew that with every episode came the risk of stroke, brain damage, heart attack, and death.

My doctors were left with little to offer. I was put on a medication that kept my heart rate slow and my blood pressure low. This was done so that when I did go into A-Fib at least my heart wouldn't race at extraordinary high levels. Armed only with this one prescription medication and advice regarding stress and diet, I was released back into life.

Life as I knew it was managing a multi-million dollar business. I knew how many people were counting on me to get this dealership up and running. I had made a commitment to the owners that I would make this happen. I didn't consider surrender at this point. I didn't consider doing anything else or anything different than I had been doing. Shortly after being dismissed from the hospital, the doctors agreed I only had to use the oxygen on an as needed basis. I had probably grown accustomed to the breathing difficulty. Using the oxygen didn't seem necessary to me. I was back to work less than two weeks after my back surgery, but more significantly, less than two weeks after we discontinued the Cordarone.

All I knew to do at the time was to pray. Only God knew my predicament. He alone knew the plans He had for my life. I continued to pray for His help and guidance. I tried to cut down my hours. I met with my management staff and outlinined for them what my hours would be from that point on. I believe I actually adhered to that schedule for all of two weeks. After that it was pretty much "back in the saddle again" and I charged ahead.

The weeks that followed were rough. My back was healing, my pain was extreme, and my energy level was poor. With the passing of time I realized I hadn't had an A-Fib episode. I had fully expected it. I was walking on egg shells, geared up for it, making plans of how I would handle it, and here it was two or three weeks later and no A-Fib. I couldn't believe it. I wasn't taking any preventative medication at this point and yet I was seemingly free of arrhythmia. At my next doctor's visit, I shared my good news. He explained to me that Cordarone stays in the tissues of your body for a long time. It's a drug that hangs on, even after you discontinue taking it. He wasn't surprised by my brief reprieve. He said it would take 3-6 months for the medication to be completely out of my system. So even though I had discontinued taking it every day, it was still there...I guess this was a good thing. It gave me some time.

I was taken off Cordarone in December. It was now July 4th. I had plans with my ex-husband to go for a drive and see the fire works that night. It was nice that we could be friends. It was good we could actually make plans to see each other once in a while. As I got out of the shower that morning it hit me. You know you never really think about your heart, this vital little muscle that keeps your body functioning from head to toe, this organ the size of your fist, this pumping, beating, incomprehensible machine that keeps every fiber of your being operating around the clock 24 hours a day. Like a car that starts every time you turn the key and runs perfectly when out on the road, you don't dwell on the inner workings, or the miraculous way it was put together. You don't, that is, until it doesn't start or until it misses or sputters. Then you can think of nothing else. It's the same with the heart...it gets little attention or thought until it doesn't do what we expect it to, or what we take for granted that it will do. I felt it rumble. I grabbed the door frame. I prayed. *Oh, no, Lord..not now, please don't let this start again...please, Lord.* I sat down. Maybe it was a fluke...maybe it would pass; maybe not. It persisted with a vengeance. It had been three years. I didn't know if I was just not accustomed to it or if it was actually worse than I had remembered. I couldn't catch my breath. I had to lie down. In a few minutes I tried to reach Dennis. He would have to make a long drive and I wanted to let him know I wouldn't be able to go today. I had hoped to reach him before he left his house. As it turned out I did not and he was there within the hour. We took our drive. It was just a bit shorter than we planned. We drove to the emergency room. *Oh, Lord, I thought these days were behind me. I thought I wouldn't have to do this anymore. Why, Why?* The nurse at the front desk took my pulse rate and didn't take the time to proceed with the check- in procedures. She called someone on the staff and they rushed me back into a room. It was a scene with which I was all too familiar. I knew what to expect. I was hooked up to monitors, an IV was started, technicians came to do an EKG and a chest X-Ray. My cardiologist was called. Medications were administered. Thankfully by nightfall I had converted back to sinus rhythm. I had all the fireworks I could handle for one day. I went straight home and to bed.

July 5th I reported for work as usual. There was a difference today though. Today I knew there was no hedge left. My time had run out. With no medication remaining in my system, I was on my own from this point on. Every day for the next year I faced each morning worried about what the day would bring. Before my feet hit the floor I asked the Lord for help and strength. I prayed every day for a cure. I cried most every night. I lived in fear.

Despite the mental and physical strain I was under, the company got the very best part of me. The business was successful. We were profitable and some months we were even out performing our mother store. That was a great victory for me personally. The real victories during those years, however, were the relationships made with the people I worked with. They were indeed a very special group. They touched my life and played a big part in helping me maintain my momentum.

In January of the next year I brought all my projections to the table. I was excited about the new year, about the opportunity to, once again, set goals and discuss strategies. I was still consumed by my job and lost in the identity of 'General Manager', but this giant balloon of success I had blown up for myself was beginning to lose air. I was unsure how long I could physically continue this pace. The pressures were great; the expectations were greater. The down-side of great achievement is that the bench mark keeps rising.

At this particular point in my life I was living in denial and probably defiance. I had been faced several times now with my own mortality. It seemed as soon as one crisis came to closure, another would develop. It left me hard. I felt like tragedy was lurking behind every corner, lying in wait, strategically planning to take me down. But still I forged ahead. I dug my own personal fox hole; continued playing the part of a tough soldier, loading my guns and lining up my weapons, egging it on.

My health wasn't the only issue at this point in time. I was beginning to ask myself some crucial and sobering questions about where I was going with my life. I had been chasing fulfillment based on my job, my performance, and earnings, but God wanted me to base my worth on my relationship with Him. He wasn't at all impressed with my obsession to show strength and self-sufficiency. He wanted me to face my weaknesses, admit my frailty and rely on Him. In time...little did I know it then...I would embrace my real identity, that of "Child of the King."

In my prayer journals during that time I recorded over and over again, "Hold me in your arms, dear God. Strengthen me...uphold me with Your mighty right hand." I prayed with my pen, "Bless me indeed, draw me to Yourself." I knew there was unknown territory ahead and I prayed that God would prepare me.

I would need to back away from my job before my performance declined. It was simply a matter of time. All I knew to do was stay in the battle as long as I was able. The war inside me raged and the questions roared.

A Little Deeper

Have you been there? Have you faced a time in your life when you were spiraling toward destruction and you responded by trying to out-run the problem?

Gideon threw out his "fleece" several times, testing God's voice and God's will. How do you discern God's voice and His will in your life?

Moses prayed in Exodus 33:13,

"If You are pleased with me, teach me Your ways so I may know You and continue to find favor with You.

153

James 1:5 tells us,

> "If any of you lacks wisdom, he should ask God, who gives
> generously to all without finding fault,
> and it will be given to him."

"Dear God, I long to know Your heart. Give me wisdom to discern your perfect will for my life. Draw me close. Teach me your way."

NINTEEN

RUN!

"The Lord is my rock,
my fortress and my deliverer."
Psalm 18:2

There's rarely just one battle to deal with. In our fallen world there are usually several skirmishes going on at once. The war was raging in my life, encompassing battlegrounds beyond my own personal health and career issues.

My oldest son, Michael moved to the west coast and had been estranged from me for more than two years. We hadn't spoken; I didn't know where he was or how to reach him. I knew he was struggling with drug addiction and alcohol abuse and I felt sure this painful stretch of time, with no word from him, was an indication that he was sinking further into the depths of his dependency. Where he was geographically wasn't the biggest issue. He was out of my reach emotionally and that was the hardest part. I prayed for him every day. I begged the Lord to help him, keep him safe, turn his life around, and bring him home. I blamed myself for his problems. Evidently I hadn't been a good mother, a strong influence, or a godly example. I grieved over him for years...grieved for the wasted life, grieved because of the hurt that separated he and his family, grieved for the pain and loneliness I imagined he was suffering. I grieved because I wasn't able to 'fix' him.

The last I'd heard, he was somewhere in California in the Hollywood or Palm Springs area. I scheduled a business trip to San Francisco in March of 2001 so I made arrangements to stay a few days longer. My plan was to hire a private investigator and somehow, some way, I was going to find my son. God knew my heart, He knew my hurt and as it turned out He spared me the painful and expensive search.

I took a call one day at work and when I answered there was nothing but silence on the other end. Instantly I pulled my mind away from the demands of my job and focused on the call. Instinctively, I knew it was Michael...I was sure it was. I had answered with my normal greeting, "This is Nancy." Now, I said, "Hello, Hello." I waited but there was only silence and then the click that told me we were disconnected. When I laid down my receiver, I could feel the tears on my face. I walked around the building several times to pull myself together. Obviously whoever was on the other end of the phone had asked specifically for me. And, obviously it could have been anyone...there could have been countless explanations. But in my heart, I knew it was Michael. I prayed. I worried. I fretted. And in the end I waited.

Two days later another call came and again silence was the only response to my greeting. I said hello twice, maybe three times. I was so afraid he would hang up again. "Mike, is that you? I've waited so long to hear from you. I'll wait until you're ready to talk to me, just please don't hang up." The silence was deafening.

Then finally I heard his voice, "Hi Mom...Yeah, it's me."

I was trying desperately to keep my voice from breaking, "Oh, Michael, thank God you called. How are you? Are you okay?" He didn't hedge.

"No, Mom, I'm not." His voice was weak.

"Michael, what's going on? Are you in trouble? Do you need help? Tell me what to do. Do you need me?" He was crying. My heart was breaking. What kind of trouble was he in? What should I do? I waited. Again... the silence was horrible. I was on pins and needles... afraid he would hang up.

"I'm in trouble, mom, I'm really messed up."

I didn't think he could bring himself to say the words so I rushed in, "Is it drugs? Are you in trouble with drugs?"

This was so terribly hard for him. He tried to regain composure, "Yeah, I'm in bad shape." I said I would come and get him. He didn't want that. I pleaded with him to come home. I told him I would buy him a plane ticket and he wouldn't let me do that. I told him if he would just come I would get him help. To my surprise he finally agreed. He said he would tie up some loose ends, buy a bus ticket, and get back to me.

I believed him but was worried that tomorrow things would look different to him and he would change his mind. I have always been pretty naive about drugs, but one thing I did know was that logical thinking for the drug user wasn't the norm. I still didn't have an address or a phone number. I didn't sleep, I couldn't focus. I was an absolute wreck until I got the next call. I passed on something his dad had said, "You're running for you life son, just run, don't worry about your furniture, your clothes, your belongings, just get on that bus and run." I wish Michael's dad could have said the words to him himself, but instead I merely reiterated what I believed was good advice. Later Michael said that hearing those words spoken aloud was the confirmation he had been praying for. He had already sensed the voice of God urging him to do that very thing, "JUST RUN... DON'T LOOK BACK... JUST RUN."

He arrived with only what he wore on his back and with what he could carry in a small duffel bag. I picked him up in the middle of the night at a dark bus station. I wasn't sure it was him. It had been so long. I reached out to hug him and literally held skin and bones in my arms. I had never seen him so thin. He was gaunt. His color was ashen. But he was here, in my arms. God (and I) had another chance to fix him, to help him...this time things were going to be different; this time things were going to work out.

My focus was now on Michael and his healing. I didn't share with him how ill I was. My struggles had once again become a guarded secret.

Every day I prayed that Mike would get better. I prayed for his healing. I prayed for him to be freed from these horrifying chains of addiction. I wanted to mark the victories for my sake and for Mike's sake. I began to keep a journal, making note of the visible changes. I watched as his mind began to clear and his emotions leveled out. I didn't have a clue how to help him. I prayed that somehow my love would be enough. I listened. I calmed him when he cried. I held him when his body shook with tremors. I told him over and over again I loved him and more importantly that God loved him. I promised him God had a special and specific plan for his life. I assured him of his worth and his value. And because that's all I knew to do, I prayed it would be enough. I prayed...I prayed.

There were times I was afraid for him. There were times I was afraid of him. He was so wounded by life, so scarred by the road he had traveled. I had never doubted his salvation. He accepted the Lord as his Savior when he was a child. I believed God's Word. I believed that Michael's salvation was entirely intact, not based on his choices or actions, but based on the love and mercy of the Lord Jesus Christ. Once we are born into the family of God, nothing can separate us from His love. I knew that the Lord was rejoicing even more than I to see him "come home again." God used Michael's journey to remind me that we all need to run from "our chains" to the merciful arms of Jesus.

Satan tells us the lie that we have been too wicked, we have failed too many times, we have totally blown it, and we've run out of chances. He infects us with so much guilt that we're ashamed to come home, afraid we're not welcome. That lie builds a wall so high and so wide some people spend a lifetime never bothering to look for the "Door."

God knows we're not perfect people. He knows us better than we know ourselves. He saw our despair...He saw our need and sent His only Son to make things right. Please don't believe the lies of Satan. Don't allow guilt to keep you from the Lord. He longs for us to reach out to Him and to fellowship with Him. He wants to have a relationship with us. He wants us to come home. He is the "Door" and you will always find it open. God is waiting...waiting for you. Come home.

It's okay to admit failure. God knows your heart. He knows your shame. Psalm 56:8 says He records your tears. He's your Abba Father. He wants to make it better. He wants to help. Come home.

A Little Deeper

Meditate on the following Scripture:

Ps 18: 2-6 "The Lord is my rock, my fortress and my deliverer; my God is my rock, in whom I take refuge. He is my shield and the horn of my salvation, my stronghold.

I call to the Lord who is worthy of praise and I am saved from my enemies.

The cords of death entangled me, the torrents of destruction overwhelmed me.

The cords of the grave coiled around me, the snares of death confronted me.

In my distress I called to the Lord; I cried to my God for help. From his temple he heard my voice; my cry came before him, into his ears."

Now Praise God!

"Thank You, Dear Lord, that You love our children even more than we do. Thank You that even though I didn't always know where my son was, You knew. I will forever praise You for Your shepherd heart...He belonged to You and You didn't leave Him alone, afraid, and separated from the safety of Your shelter. Thank You, precious Lord. I pray his life will from this point be a testimony of praise for all You've done!"

TWENTY

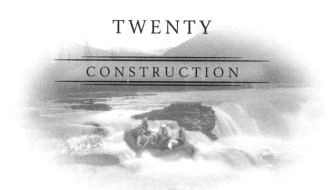

CONSTRUCTION

"There is surely a future hope for you,
and your hope will not be cut off."
Proverbs 23:18

Anyone who has ever lived in Wyoming would agree that it is a state of only two seasons. In Wyoming you have winter and when you're not having winter you have construction. As winter gives up its hold, construction equipment comes out of hiding. It shows up along the shoulders of the roads and highways, accompanied by at least 10 or 20 workers all dressed in orange vests and hard hats. They bring out all the neon signs; they build barricades and set up barrels; they put out all the flashing lights and flaggers are posted everywhere along your route to anywhere. In some sick way this parade of activity brought relief. To see all the commotion marked the end of the cold, the wind, and the snow. Relief was short-lived, however, and was soon replaced with impatience and downright agitation as the CONSTRUCTION season roared into full swing.

For me the worst part about construction is the inconvenience; it throws you off your schedule because you're forced to slow down. It's frustrating because the signs warning you to reduce your speed begin 10 to 15 miles before you really see anybody actually working on the road. But, I guess at least you're forewarned. You have plenty of time to work up an attitude, and then time to surrender that attitude and come to grips with the fact that it's out of your hands and there's nothing you can do about it. After dealing with the wide range of emotions, you finally reach the construction zone where in all probability, you're going to have to come to a full stop and wait to be waved on.

Road construction is always bothersome; the timing is bad, and the mess is unbelievable. You recognize that "down the road"...(no pun intended), things will be better. It will be much better when the pot holes are filled, when the two lanes become four, when they widen the exit and when that back road is finally paved. Oh yeah, it's hard now, but it'll be worth the inconvenience in the long run. I have to believe that a whole bunch of people, a whole bunch smarter than I am, sat around a planning table somewhere and decided what needed to be done. I have to keep telling myself that they know what they're doing.

In the early spring of 2002, God began to post construction signs along the highways of my life. He had a huge project in mind for me. I knew I was being urged to slow down and take another road and I was aggravated because the road of my choosing had become impassable. God was leading me into a new construction season of my life, and the work was about to begin. Just like in road construction, sometimes it has to get worse before it can get better. The job is messy. It rips and tears away at what we know, what we're used to, what seems logical and

involved with my care had said it, some more compassionately than others. My days were numbered. It was "Russian Roulette" minus the revolver. Which episode would be the one to cause a stroke, another heart attack? What day would bring the final beat of my heart? I went to Pennsylvania determined to make whatever was left the best it could be.

As we stood in the driveway for the last time I felt numb; it didn't seem real. I was in a fog. Nothing was crystal clear, the way I like it. So much had transpired. I had resigned from my job, sold my dream house, watched my possessions being loaded into a trailer and now, here I was listening to my two sons map out the route we would take. As we set out on our journey, Michael was at the point, leading our little caravan east. I was the second in line and Matthew was close behind driving a moving truck that we had rented. I knew we were headed for Pennsylvania, but in my heart of hearts I felt as if my real destination was for parts 'unknown'. The boys teased me about being alone in my car for 24 hours with no one to talk to. As it turned out, it was a wonderful opportunity to be alone with God. I cried, I sang, I worshipped and praised, but mostly I just prayed. *Oh, Lord, I don't do unknowns well. You know me. I'm a get-it-done, can handle it personality. I'm so out of my comfort zone here. I don't have any answers. I don't know how this will all work, financially. I don't know what's going to happen physically. I don't know if I can deal emotionally. I don't know...I don't know...I don't know...*

Help me, Lord, to zero in on the few things I do know... I know you love me. I know you died on the cross for me. I know I'm saved. I know you've prepared a place for me in heaven. I know that by all human estimation, I should al-

ready be dead. I know that you have surely spared me for a reason. I trust you... I want to trust you more. I'm tired.. just so tired. I need to rest. I want to rest, just curl up in your arms. I trust you to take care of me. Please replace my fear with courage. Replace my doubt with hope. I hope...I hope...

A Little Deeper

In Acts 20: 22, Paul writes to the Ephesian Elders. He says, "I am going to Jerusalem, not knowing what will happen to me there." In these 'going- without- knowing' verses we can gain priceless insight from Paul's honest admission. This trip across country was definitely a 'going without knowing' experience for me. My life had been marked with adversity and hardship as far back as I could remember and now I was on a road leading me out of the limelight into seclusion...out of command into the rank and file...out of security into uncertainty. But God is Faithful!

Read:

2 Thessalonians 3:3
Hebrews 10:23
Psalm 146:6
1 Corinthians 10:13

"Lord, direct me in the path of your commands, for I know if I'm there, I will find delight (Ps 119:35) I praise You for Your faithfulness to me. I ask that You go before me now and prepare my way. It is enough that You know the end from the beginning. I place my trust and hope in YOU!"

TWENTY-ONE

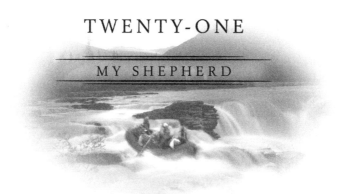

MY SHEPHERD

"Show me your way, O Lord, teach me your paths; guide
me in your truth and teach me,
for you are God my Savior,
and my hope is in you all day long."
Psalm 25:4

Matt had lived in Pennsylvania for 7 years. He and
his wife, Dana had planted a church in Cranberry Township a year earlier. They found a house for me in Cranberry. It was crying out for TLC but surprisingly that
didn't put me in a tailspin. Michael had completely orchestrated my move, personally packing every single household item, big and small. Six months earlier he had come
to me, emaciated, ill, and running from drug addiction.
He needed me to be there for him then, but now the
tables were turned. He was there for me. I counted my
blessings. I would get to live near Matt and Dana and be
with my three grandchildren, and Michael would be there
as well. I was going to be able to hear Matthew preach on
Sunday mornings. I could continue to watch Michael get
stronger and healthier and more importantly watch him
draw nearer to God.

On the other hand, my heart was breaking because

Mandy was in Colorado. That part made no sense. *Lord, how can I leave her?* I must have asked the Lord that question at least a hundred times. It made no sense to me, it wasn't logical. It seemed so backwards, but I had made a commitment to trust God, no matter what. Somehow he gave me peace that everything would work out, everything would come full circle.

When I moved to Pennsylvania from the Colorado/ Wyoming area, I missed the sun. Colorado ranks high on the list for the number of sunshine days per year. The Pennsylvania clouds were massive and constant. I hadn't realized there would be such a difference and the drastic weather change was a hard adjustment. In the beginning I would sit down and reason that it wasn't so bad. I would even get out a paper and pen and do the old "Ben Franklin," listing the pros and cons of the situation. On the pro side I would always list the beauty of trees, and the green lushness of Pennsylvania. Although Colorado has a lot of evergreen trees and tons of aspen trees in the mountain areas, the flat land along the front range is actually dry and the trees are sparse. There were plants that grew wild in my yard in Pennsylvania that I had tried and tried to grow as house plants in Colorado. I love the greenery. But, do you know what makes it green? Do you know why the trees are so beautiful? Of course the answer to both those questions is RAIN. With rain comes clouds and, yes, with clouds, less sunshine. At first I was troubled that the house Matt found for me didn't have a sprinkler system. I soon realized there was little need in Pennsylvania for such trivial equipment.

Somewhere I read the statement, "all sunshine makes a desert." A little rain had been planned for me and even though I resisted, it made me greener, healthier, more vibrant spiritually. I learned to collapse in the arms of Jesus when the clouds closed in. It was sweet relief. I'd never thought I'd had any one to take care of me, anyone I could count on, any one to lean on. Now in my early fifties I was learning that Jesus stood waiting for me to turn to Him for that care and consolation. During this season of my life I prayed more often, more intently. I had such an unquenchable, deep desire just to know the heart of God. These were hard times. These were fearful times. I'm so thankful that during these valleys, bitterness didn't drive me away from the Lord. I'm thankful that my fear, severe illness, discouragement, and depression have instead driven me deeper into the arms of Jesus. I praise Him for that. I've learned to love what the rain brings in Pennsylvania. I've learned to recognize and appreciate what hard times bring in my heart and life as a child of God. I grow in the valleys. I flourish in the rain.

Living out God's Word...

The Lord is my shepherd. I shall not be in want. He makes me lie down in green pastures.

In this season of my life the Lord truly was asking me to slow down...lie down in His green pastures. He was drawing me aside, sweetly watching over me, caring for me, planning and orchestrating the path ahead.

He leads me beside the quiet waters.

Like Elijah coming out of the limelight, retreating for a time to the Kerith Ravine, this was my brook. (I Kings 17:3-4). I had been snatched away from what I thought was 'my' world. God was saying, "Come away...get alone.

Let go of those things that feed your pride and ego.
Come live by the brook."

He restores my soul.

God daily saturated my heart with a peace like I've
never known before.

He guides me in paths of righteousness for His name's sake.

Truly He has my best interest in mind. He knows my
needs.

He goes before me, preparing the way.

He works His best in me and continues to guide me to
a place of maturity so that my life can bring Him honor
and glory.

Even though I walk through the valley of the shadow of death, I will fear no evil, for you are with me. Your rod and your staff, they comfort me.

It had been impressed on me that with each episode I
was at extremely high risk for stroke, heart attack, and
death. I was having 3 to 5 episodes a week even at the
lower altitude. There was no comfort outside the Lord.
He was my refuge and my strength. I shared with Him
every day that I didn't want to die, I wasn't ready to die,
but if that was what this day would bring, if that was
His will, I would surrender my will. I prayed that He
wouldn't let go of my hand. I prayed that my passing
would be like crossing the street when I was a child. My
dad held my hand so tight it almost hurt. I knew he
wouldn't let go. I want to cross over into heaven just

like that, hand in hand with my heavenly father. That was my daily prayer...all day long.

You prepare a table before me in the presence of my enemies. You anoint my head with oil, my cup overflows.

The Lord blessed me immeasurably. Worries and problems that screamed at me and plagued me were miraculously settled one by one. When I made the move out east I had no idea of how my finances would work out. I didn't know how to apply for Social Security disability. I didn't know what I was going to do about health insurance. I didn't have a doctor in Pennsylvania. I had no one that knew me or my medical background, no one to call in an emergency. So many questions...

Surely goodness and love will follow me all the days of my life and I will dwell in the house of the Lord forever.

The Lord bountifully provided over the next few months. When I left my employment my company provided only local health coverage and I had no option of a policy that would be honored out of state. Because of my health issues, finding affordable insurance coverage was impossible. When I moved to Pennsylvania, I believed I had no health coverage at all. Yet one month after I left, the automobile business changed providers. Because I was still under their umbrella, I was able to pay a Cobra premium and the new insurance company would honor out of state services. Was that a miracle God worked out just for me? I believe it was! I trusted God to provide and He did! God met all my need in miraculous ways! What a God of wonders He is!

171

A Little Deeper

Pray God's Word. Use the 23rd Psalm and break it down into sections, and make each word applicable to your own life. Spend some time...write it in your journal. Make it your personal prayer. It will change your perspective.

Consider these verses as well:

Isaiah 26:12   Psalm 115:15
Psalm 84:12   Proverbs 16:20
Proverbs 23:18   Romans 15:13

"Thank You, dear Lord for Your goodness to me. I know Your hand is upon my life. I need only look at all the problems You have solved, all the painful areas You have touched, all the hurts You have healed. I can see that the rain doesn't come to ruin me but to shape me. Thank You for the rain that causes me to run for the shelter only You can provide."

TWENTY-TWO

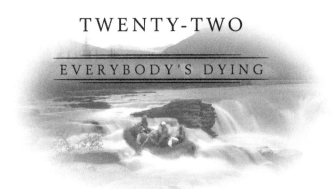

EVERYBODY'S DYING

I cry aloud to the Lord; I lift up my voice to the Lord for mercy.
I pour out my complaint before Him;
before Him I tell my trouble."
Psalm 142:1-2

In March of 2003, Mandy moved to Pennsylvania. I had been so torn about leaving her in Colorado, but the Lord provided a job for her and she came running. What a blessing to live near all of my three children and three grandchildren. The Lord was granting me this precious and priceless time. Still, in many ways we were all waiting for the other "shoe to fall." I was acutely aware that I was probably living my last days. I know I wasn't the only one living under the pressure. My children were ever vigilant, ever close, and ever watchful.

In Genesis 37 we find the story of Joseph. He was favored by his father because he was the baby. He had been born when his father, Jacob, was an old man. I'm sure he wasn't all that different from the other sons. He wasn't more handsome, more intelligent or witty, he just showed up on the scene when his daddy was more mature. Joseph's brothers were jealous of him because they sensed their father loved him more, loved him differently than he had loved them. You know the story; their jealousy led them to fake a famous crime scene. They threw Joseph in a cistern and dipped his coat in goat's blood. They presented the blood soaked garment to his father, leading him to believe that Joseph had been killed by a ferocious animal. They sold him to Midianite merchants who took him to Egypt and resold him to Potiphar. Joseph's brothers wrote him off. He was out of their lives, out of sight, out of mind. He was forgotten by his siblings and mourned by his father. As the years passed, there wasn't anyone looking for him, no one in hot pursuit to rescue him.

As the story unfolds, we see Joseph estranged from his family, exiled from his home and thrown into unfamiliar and undeserving circumstances. He was alone, forsaken, cheated. Yet God was there, right there all the time, at work in Joseph's life and in Joseph's circumstances. The story culminates at the end of Genesis with a verse found in chapter 50, verse 20. Speaking to his brothers who are now bowed before him, asking for help and forgiveness, Joseph says, "You intended to harm me, but God intended it for good to accomplish what is now being done."

I've always wondered if Joseph had those admirable insights during the valleys of his journey, or if the full picture actually came to him down the road as he looked back. Was he able to say, "God intended this for good" when he was misunderstood and mistreated, when he was abused, when he was afraid, destitute, cold, hungry and ill? Or did his great resolve and wisdom develop after the rushing of the rapids widened into calmer waters.

For me, it's not always clear, especially during the

roughest waters, to be able to say with absolute conviction that I know God is at work in my life and the hard times are part of His design for my good.

The next months of my life were shrouded in confusion and fear. This disease of mine was undeniably out of control. I thought that moving to Pennsylvania would make things better. I left the demands of my high stress job. I moved to a lower altitude. I rested every day. I tried to stay calm and carefree. I was doing everything I knew to change my lifestyle. I so wanted to be better. I found new doctors in Pennsylvania who were as baffled as the doctors I had left in Colorado. We tried an old medicine, one I had taken years earlier, hoping to wring a few months of reprieve out of it. It didn't help my problem; it actually initiated another.

One Sunday morning while getting ready for church I went into an unusually severe episode of A-fib. My heart rate was way too fast. I was wearing a monitor prescribed by my cardiologist so I was able to record my heart rhythms. As I recall, I pushed the record button three or four times that day. I felt so miserable I didn't get around to calling the recordings in until Monday morning. Ten minutes after sending the recordings over, I got a call from my cardiologist's office. The nurse asked if I was okay.

I said, "Well, No, I'm not okay. I'm really sick." "We know," she said. "The heart center just sent over your last recordings. Nancy, the monitor showed Ventricular Tachycardia. This is bad. The doctor wants to talk to you." Strange as it may sound, I wasn't familiar with Ventricular Tachycardia. I had become an expert on Atrial Fibrillation and the other list of arrhythmias I had been labeled with, but this one was new to me.

The doctor came on the phone. "Nancy, where are you right now?"

"Uh, in the family room," I answered.

"Listen to me, don't take any more Rythmol. You've been in and out of Ventricular Tachycardia. The electrophysiologist and I think the medication is possibly the cause. Is there someone there with you?"

"Not right now," I answered. "What do you want me to do?"

He asked me to send in another strip immediately. After he got it he called back and said to come in to his office. I saw him that day and several days in a row after that. He told me the strips were alarming. The recordings showed I had been in and out of both Ventricular Tachycardia, Ventricular Fibrillation and Flutter. He further informed me that these were life-threatening arrhythmias and more often than not they lead to sudden cardiac death. He made it clear I was a walking miracle.

I had traveled this road before. I had sat in an office much like this one. I had listened as other Doctors said similar things. I should be dead but I was alive...alive...yet there was little time to rejoice because the warnings seemed to overshadow the miracle.

After wearing the monitor for another four weeks the determination was made that the Rythmol was the cause of things going from bad to worse and a further decision was made to never prescribe any kind of arrhythmia medication for me again.

What frustration! The one medicine that helped me was destroying my lungs and liver. All other similar medications had now been ruled out because of the probability of causing even deadlier problems. I was so discouraged.

This felt so unfair. Death felt so eminent. On the other hand I knew there were things worse than dying. I prayed every day I wouldn't have a stroke and be left in a helpless state, a vegetable, an unresponsive, dependent burden for my family. In the depths of my frustration, God gave me encouragement, a new perspective that helped me see my terminal situation in a new light. I realized that everyone, every single person on the face of this earth is, in fact, dying. From the moment we are born we begin the dying process. In the long run, I was really no different than anybody else.

In an effort to be optimistic, my Doctors would always leave me with a statement like, "There's new research on the horizon. We'll keep you abreast of any new developments." I don't know if there was any truth in their statements or if there was just nothing else left to say. But I did my best to grab on to hope. I began to read, read, read and study, study, study. I collected every piece of literature, every testimonial, and every article I could find relative to my disease. I got involved in posting questions on the web, comparing situations, medical approaches and processes. I needed to believe that somehow, somewhere, something would happen... something good....I so needed something good.

A Little Deeper

Has there been a time in your life when hope seemed lost? Did you find yourself surrendering to the situation or were you able to side step the negative, dodge the logical and stay on course?

Do you find yourself having to dig for hope, needing to use it as a quick fix tool to eradicate the despair that's running rampant?

Where do you find the strength to hope...where is your stronghold? WHO is your stronghold?

Psalm 27:1 "The Lord is my salvation—whom shall I fear? The Lord is the stronghold of my life—of whom shall I be afraid?"

Psalm 42:5 "Why are you downcast, O my soul? Why so disturbed within me? Put your hope in God...praise Him, my Savior and my God."

Read:

Romans 15:13
Romans 12:12
Psalm 71:5

I Timothy 6:17
Psalm 31:24
Romans 15:4

"Dear Lord Jesus, You are my hope. Wrap me in your arms...hold me tight. Replace my anxiety with Your perfect peace. Give me courage to face tomorrow and hope to carry me through the day. I love You Lord!"

TWENTY-THREE

HELLO HOPE!

"But as far as me, I will always have hope;
I will praise you more and more."
Psalm 71:14

The internet is a phenomenal tool, but when using it as an educational source for medical issues, it can be a two-edged sword. I navigated my way through hundreds of medical search engines every day. My pursuit of this "new hope on the horizon" was exhausting. I was desperate to find new treatment, new medication, new enthusiasm and new energy. All too often, my pursuit left me with more questions and a greater level of fear than I had to begin with.

I kept reading about a new heart procedure, an on the edge, experimental laser surgery being offered to end-of-the-road Arrhythmia patients. The most complete, comprehensive write up available was put out by the Cleveland Clinic. I found it pretty interesting that here I was only two hours from the Cleveland Clinic.

I spoke to my cardiologist about the surgery. He was honest enough to say he didn't know too much about it but would check into it for me. After doing some homework he reported back, saying I'm probably not a good candidate. He reminded me that most heart surgeries are both pre-empted by and followed up with blood thinners. That's always the issue that disqualifies me.

I've tried to put it out of my mind but I keep thinking...*maybe...maybe there's a way.* Today Michael is driving me to Cleveland. I want to talk to the research staff. I have to ask the surgeons if there is any chance they would consider me for this program. I'm sitting here with all my records in my lap. I'm resisting the urge to read through the countless pages, and study the tests results one more time. I've seen it all. Rehearsing it again would only discourage me, and I can't handle any more opposition right now. So I choose not to thumb through the stack of papers. I choose instead to hope.

My Hope

The river rages, the rapids are high
The water is deep, clouds hang in the sky
Sinking deeper, gasping for air
A picture painted...life in despair

Courage defeated by darkness of night
Strength taken captive; no help in sight
Fear takes the reins, still there's hope within...
That spirit that struggles and longs to win.

A seed of hope planted in your heart and mine
Nurtured and watered through the tests of time
Pushing its way through the darkness and dirt
Believing the better and healing the hurt.

Hope's name is Jesus, O Praise His Dear Name
Into my wandering life He came
He drew me, He bought me, He saved my soul
He touched my heart and made me whole

I was not snatched from the throes of dread
He carries me through those deep waters instead
My lifeline, my anchor on stormy sea
My sail, my wind, my sun is He...

In the arms of Jesus I find great peace
When the rivers rage and the waters are deep
He gives me strength when the storms are strong
He gives me rest when my journey is long

Yes Hope has a name so precious and true
It's Master and Lord, and Comforter too
My Redeemer, my Savior, Counselor and Friend
I will cling to my Hope 'til the very end.

by Nancy Kaltenberger

Hope Speaks

Romans 15:4
For everything that was written in the past was written to teach us, so that through endurance and the encouragement of the Scriptures we might have hope.

Romans 15:13
May the God of hope fill you with all joy and peace as you trust in him, so that you may overflow with hope by the power of the Holy Spirit.

Job 11:18
You will be secure, because there is hope; you will look about you and take your rest in safety.

Job 13:15
Though he slay me, yet will I hope in him.

Psalm 25:3
No one whose hope is in you will ever be put to shame…

Psalm 25:5
guide me in your truth and teach me, for you are God my Savior, and my hope is in you all day long.

Psalm 25:21
May integrity and uprightness protect me, because my hope is in you.

Psalm 31:24
Be strong and take heart, all you who hope in the LORD.

Psalm 33:18
But the eyes of the LORD are on those who fear him, on those whose hope is in his unfailing love

Psalm 33:20
We wait in hope for the LORD; he is our help and our shield.

Psalm 33:22
May your unfailing love rest upon us, O LORD, even as we put our hope in you.

Psalm 37:9
For evil men will be cut off, but those who hope in the LORD will inherit the land.

Psalm 39:7
"But now, Lord, what do I look for? My hope is in you.

Psalm 42:5, Psalm 42:11, Psalm 43:5
Why are you downcast, O my soul? Why so disturbed within me? Put your hope in God, for I will yet praise him, my Savior and my God.

Psalm 52:9
I will praise you forever for what you have done; in your name I will hope, for your name is good. I will praise you in the presence of your saints.

Psalm 62:5
Find rest, O my soul, in God alone; my hope comes from him.

Psalm 65:5
You answer us with awesome deeds of righteousness, O God our Savior, the hope of all the ends of the earth and of the farthest seas,

Psalm 71:5
For you have been my hope, O Sovereign LORD, my confidence since my youth.

Psalm 71:14
But as for me, I will always have hope; I will praise you more and more.

Psalm 119:49
Remember your word to your servant, for you have given me hope.

Psalm 119:74
May those who fear you rejoice when they see me, for I have put my hope in your word

Psalm 119:81
My soul faints with longing for your salvation, but I have put my hope in your word

Psalm 119:114
You are my refuge and my shield; I have put my hope in your word.

Psalm 119:147
I rise before dawn and cry for help; I have put my hope in your word.

Psalm 130:5
I wait for the LORD, my soul waits, and in his word I put my hope.

Psalm 130:7
O Israel, put your hope in the LORD, for with the LORD is unfailing love and with him is full redemption.

Psalm 131:3
O Israel, put your hope in the LORD both now and forevermore.

Psalm 146:5
Blessed is he whose help is the God of Jacob, whose hope is in the LORD his God,

Psalm 147:11
the LORD delights in those who fear him, who put their hope in his unfailing love.

Proverbs 13:12
Hope deferred makes the heart sick, but a longing fulfilled is a tree of life.

Proverbs 23:18
There is surely a future hope for you, and your hope will not be cut off.

Proverbs 24:14
Know also that wisdom is sweet to your soul; if you find it, there is a future hope for you, and your hope will not be cut off.

Ecclesiastes 9:4
Anyone who is among the living has hope —even a live dog is better off than a dead lion!

Isaiah 40:31
...but those who hope in the LORD will renew their strength. They will soar on wings like eagles; they will run and not grow weary, they will walk and not be faint.

Isaiah 49:23
I am the LORD; those who hope in me will not be disappointed."

Jeremiah 14:22
Do any of the worthless idols of the nations bring rain? Do the skies themselves send down showers? No, it is you, O LORD our God. Therefore our hope is in you, for you are the one who does all this.

Jeremiah 29:11
For I know the plans I have for you," declares the LORD, "plans to prosper you and not to harm you, plans to give you hope and a future.

Lamentations 3:25
The LORD is good to those whose hope is in him, to the one who seeks him;

Micah 7:7
But as for me, I watch in hope for the LORD, I wait for God my Savior; my God will hear me.

Matthew 12:21
In his name the nations will put their hope."

Acts 2:26
Therefore my heart is glad and my tongue rejoices; my body also will live in hope,

Romans 5:2
through whom we have gained access by faith into this grace in which we now stand. And we rejoice in the hope of the glory of God.

Romans 5:3-5
...we know that suffering produces perseverance; perseverance, character; and character, hope. And hope does not disappoint us, because God has poured out his love into our hearts by the Holy Spirit, whom he has given us.

Romans 8:24
For in this hope we were saved. But hope that is seen is no hope at all. Who hopes for what he already has?

Romans 12:12
Be joyful in hope, patient in affliction, faithful in prayer.

1 Corinthians 15:19
If only for this life we have hope in Christ, we are to be pitied more than all men.

2 Corinthians 1:10
He has delivered us from such a deadly peril, and he will deliver us. On him we have set our hope that he will continue to deliver us

2 Corinthians 3:12
Therefore, since we have such a hope, we are very bold.

Galatians 5:5
But by faith we eagerly await through the Spirit the righteousness for which we hope.

Ephesians 1:18
I pray also that the eyes of your heart may be enlightened in order that you may know the hope to which he has called you, the riches of his glorious inheritance in the saints,

Ephesians 4:4
There is one body and one Spirit—just as you were called to one hope when you were called—

Colossians 1:27
To them God has chosen to make known among the Gentiles the glorious riches of this mystery, which is Christ in you, the hope of glory.

1 Thessalonians 1:3
We continually remember before our God and Father your work produced by faith, your labor prompted by love, and your endurance inspired by hope in our Lord Jesus Christ.

1 Timothy 4:10
(and for this we labor and strive), that we have put our hope in the living God, who is the Savior of all men, and especially of those who believe

1 Timothy 5:5
The widow who is really in need and left all alone puts her hope in God and continues night and day to pray and to ask God for help.

1 Timothy 6:17
Command those who are rich in this present world not to be arrogant nor to put their hope in wealth, which is so uncertain, but to put their hope in God, who richly provides us with everything for our enjoyment.

Titus 1:2
a faith and knowledge resting on the hope of eternal life, which God, who does not lie, promised before the beginning of time,

Titus 2:13
while we wait for the blessed hope—the glorious appearing of our great God and Savior, Jesus Christ,

Titus 3:7
so that, having been justified by his grace, we might become heirs having the hope of eternal life.

Hebrews 6:18
God did this so that, by two unchangeable things in which it is impossible for God to lie, we who have fled to take hold of the hope offered to us may be greatly encouraged.

Hebrews 10:23
Let us hold unswervingly to the hope we profess, for he who promised is faithful.

1 Peter 1:3
Praise be to the God and Father of our Lord Jesus Christ! In his great mercy he has given us new birth into a living hope through the resurrection of Jesus Christ from the dead,

1 Peter 1:21
Through him you believe in God, who raised him from the dead and glorified him, and so your faith and hope are in God.

1 Peter 3:15
But in your hearts set apart Christ as Lord. Always be prepared to give an answer to everyone who asks you to give the reason for the hope that you have. But do this with gentleness and respect,

What Some Have Said

"Nancy's authenticity and leadership savvy, has made her one of the best seminar speakers we have had at our Schools of Leadership. Nancy has the life story and relationship with the Lord that makes her a credible and wise voice for the hope that all of us need! This book will connect your heart to hope so you too might be a voice to others."

Marc V. Rutter, National Director
Human Resource Leadership
Campus Crusade for Christ

"Nancy is one of the most creative, dynamic and genuine people I have met along my ministry journey. When Nancy enters the room you just sense that good things are about to follow…and they always do. Her enthusiasm for life and her passion for God are contagious. She possesses the rare combination of visionary leadership coupled with warmth and tenderness that makes one want to be a part of whatever she is engaged in. Nancy Kaltenberger is the real deal."

Eric Swanson
Leadership Network,
Author

Nancy is a brilliant communicator and a gifted leader. Someone once asked me who my hero is and without hesitation, I answered, "My hero is my Mom." She is the reason I am in full-time ministry today. Her passion for Jesus Christ, her faithfulness to prayer, and her Godly example are a source of great inspiration in my life. The honesty and transparency captured within these pages will pierce your heart with unforgettable examples as well as indelible application.

Matthew W. Kaltenberger, Senior Pastor,
Grace Community Church, Cranberry Township, PA

Nancy is unselfish about sharing normally guarded personal experiences. That openness and vulnerability bridges a special connection with her audience as she shares the character of God and teaches Spiritual relevance.

Karen Stroupe, Ambridge, PA

Nancy is an inspiration, a gifted teacher and leader, and truly a brilliant story teller. Her life is characterized by a grace and maturity that I know was forged through years of walking close to her Savior.

Barbara Lopez, Director, Constituent Services
House of Representatives, Commonwealth of Pennsylvania

I believe Nancy's professional background enables her to deliver a relevant, clearly communicated, and cohesive message. Her stories coupled with her knowledge of Scripture will touch your heart and then bring you back full circle to the TRUTH that we all seek in our relationship with Christ and then the relationships we live out with one another..

Kim Wellington, Women's Ministry Leader
Central Christian Church, Colorado Springs, CO

The inspiration of this book will linger far beyond the turning of the last page. Nancy radiates the HOPE that lives so deeply within her core. To know her is truly to love her. There is wonderful opportunity within these pages to get acquainted with Nancy, to share her miraculous story, and be encouraged by her extraordinary account of God's faithfulness.

Dr. Libby Bailey, Elbert, CO

As wars rage around us, both in the literal sense and the more intimate personal and emotional sense, hope is something we all need. When I am facing a tough time, just having a friend who has been there and knows how I feel and who has lived through it gives me hope that I, too, can forge the raging river. *Hope When the River Rages* is like that friend, who with biblical wisdom, can come beside you with a hug and with hope.

Marita Littauer
President CLASServices Inc.
Speaker/Author, "But Lord, I Was Happy Shallow" &
"The Journey to Jesus"

About the Author

Nancy Kaltenberger recently retired from a 25 year career in the automobile industry where she served in the pinnacle position of General Manager, a role that included teaching, training, speaking, and motivating. Nancy has experienced 6 unique near-death episodes through which she loves to give an account of the mercy of God's "mighty right hand." At this *Halftime Point* of her life, Nancy is investing herself full-time in speaking and writing that will count for eternity. Nancy has taught Bible Classes and served as Guest Speaker within many church groups and organizations across the country. She served as a seminar speaker for the Campus Crusade for Christ Leadership Training Session, and has been often recruited as a featured speaker for the Business, Advertising, and Marketing Classes at Colorado State University in Fort Collins, CO.

Nancy has three grown children and 3 grandchildren. She lives in Loveland, Colorado.

Nancy's professional background, her communication and relational skills coupled with her knowledge of the Bible and her walk with the Lord come together to make Nancy one of the most genuine, relevant, and dynamic speakers in the Christian arena today. She is available for Retreats, Luncheons, Banquets, Seminars, Team Building and Recovery Events. Nancy would love to come speak at **your** event.

For More Information Contact:
Heart of Hope Ministries
Nancy Kaltenberger
970-219-9768
nk4m@comcast.net

More Books From
LifeSong Publishers

~Ancient Paths for Modern Women Series~
by Judy Gerry

"This is what the Lord says: 'Stand at the crossroads and look; ask for the
ancient paths, ask where the good way is, and walk in it,
and you will find rest for your souls.'"
(Jeremiah 6:16)

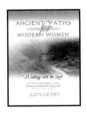 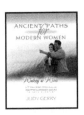 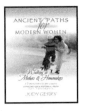 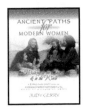

Walking With the Lord	Walking as Wives	Walking as Mothers and Homemakers	Walking in the Church and in the World
ISBN 0-9718306-2-2	ISBN 0-9718306-3-0	ISBN 0-9718306-4-9	ISBN 0-9718306-5-7
$11.99 100pp 7.5x10	$11.99 112pp 7.5x10	$11.99 110pp 7.5x10	$11.99 130pp 7.5x10

"Here is a timely, reassuring and professionally crafted study resource
which belongs in every church library and on the study agenda for
thinking women."
**Howard G. Hendricks, Distinguished Professor,
Dallas Theological Seminary**

"In a day when so many Christian women are floundering and
confused, the wisdom found in this program is timely and desperately
needed."
Nancy Leigh DeMoss, Author- Host of Revive Our Hearts Radio

A comprehensive year-long series...
A study of ancient truths that will completely
revolutionize your life!!

Baptism and Communion Preparation

God... Should I Be Baptized?
ISBN 0-9718306-1-4
$10.99 96pp 8.5x11
For children 8-12

The Lord's Supper... Let's Get Ready!
ISBN 0-9718306-6-5
$10.99 96pp 8.5x11
For children/youth 8-14

"This is a great effort that I recommend highly for churches that desire to expose their children to solid teaching on the Lord's table. "
John MacArthur,
Grace Community Church, Sun Valley, CA

God's Plan... My Response
ISBN 0-9718306-0-6
$9.99 96pp 6x9
For Jr. Hi / Hi School

To Order Contact:
LifeSong Publishers
P.O. Box 183, Somis, CA 93066
(805) 655-5644
www.LifeSongPublishers.com
email: mailbox@LifeSongPublishers.com

Notes